Managing Disruptive Behavior Workbook for Teens

A TOOLBOX of REPRODUCIBLE ASSESSMENTS and ACTIVITIES for Facilitators

Ester R.A. Leutenberg
and John J. Liptak, EdD

Duluth, Minnesota

Stress & Wellness Publishers

101 W. 2nd St., Suite 203
Duluth, MN 55802

800-247-6789

books@wholeperson.com
www.wholeperson.com

Managing Disruptive Behavior Workbook for Teens
A Toolbox of Reproducible Assessments and Activities
for Facilitators.

Copyright ©2015 by Ester R.A. Leutenberg and John Liptak.
All rights reserved. Except for short excerpts for review purposes and materials in the activities and handouts sections, no part of this workbook may be reproduced or transmitted in any form by any means, electronic or mechanical without permission in writing from the publisher. Activities and handouts are meant to be photocopied.

All efforts have been made to ensure accuracy of the information contained in this book as of the date published.
The author(s) and the publisher expressly disclaim responsibility for any adverse effects arising from the use or application of the information contained herein.

Printed in the United States of America

10 9 8 7 6 5 4 3 2 1

Editorial Director: Carlene Sippola
Art Director: Joy Morgan Dey
Assistant Art Director: Mathew Pawlak

Library of Congress Control Number: 2014957802
ISBN: 978-157025-327-0

Introduction

Managing Disruptive Behavior Workbook for Teens

Disruptive behaviors are characterized by consistent patterns of ongoing, uncooperative, defiant and hostile behaviors. With these behaviors, teens continue to "break the rules." All children break some rules, especially less important rules. More serious disruptive behavior is a normal part of maturing. Unfortunately, continued disruptive behavior negatively impacts the teen and every person the teen meets.

When teenagers are routinely disruptive, a mental health issue may be involved. As well as teaching teens the skills to identify and improve their behavior, one of the purposes of this workbook is for the facilitator to better understand teen behavior, not to diagnose it. If the facilitator believes a mental health issue is a possibility, a school counselor or trained clinician is recommended.

A Guide to Help Teens Manage Disruptive Behavior

The assessments and activities in this workbook are designed to provide facilitators with a wide variety of tools to use in helping teens learn to manage their disruptive behaviors. Many choices for self-exploration are provided for facilitators to determine which tools will help their teens overcome disruptive behaviors.

The purpose of this workbook is to provide a user-friendly guide to short-term assessments and activities designed to help teens cope with and manage the disruptive behaviors that are causing problems at school, at home, and in the community.

In addition, this workbook is designed to help provide facilitators and teens with tools and information needed to be aware of disruptive behaviors and overcome the stigma attached to them, NOT to diagnose disruptive behavior problems.

In order to help teens successfully deal with problem behaviors, it is extremely helpful for facilitators to have a variety of appealing, user-friendly assessments and activities to help teens "open-up" and begin to feel as if their problem behaviors can be identified and managed, and that they are not alone. The *Managing Disruptive Behavior Workbook for Teens* provides assessments and self-guided activities to help teens reduce the intensity of their problem behaviors, learn coping skills, and begin living more effective and fulfilling lives.

When to Worry?

Disruptive behavior problems surface in classrooms, at home and in the community as teens argue with adults, deliberately disobey reasonable requests from adults, fight with peers, experience increased moodiness, having trouble controlling their temper, and underachieve in school. Extreme disruptive behaviors tend to become more intense and longer lasting than typical behaviors of most teens.

The good news is that facilitators can help teens learn to make small changes that will result in major shifts in their behavior, as well as to utilize many of the strategies in this workbook to reduce the intensity and number of disruptive behavior problems that teens will experience. Teens can develop the cognitive, affective, and behavioral skills needed to decrease the amount, depth and duration of their disruptive behavior and begin to feel a sense of joy, contentment, and wellbeing. **Teens who experience these problem behaviors for an extended period of time are at risk of having a serious behavior or adjustment problem and need to seek a trained clinician.**

How Does Disruptive Behavior Manifest Itself?

In teens, disruptive behavior emerge in a wide variety of ways. It is critical to be aware of and to understand how these symptoms are commonly observed in teens. While all symptoms may not be present in everything, symptoms that do surface can cause significant distress and/or impairment in daily functioning at home, in school, and within their community. These symptoms cause distress to the teens themselves and to the people around them.

Possible Symptoms:

- Abuses alcohol and other dangerous substances
- Acts out
- Angers easily
- Annoys others deliberately
- Assaults others verbally, physically
- Attempts or contemplates suicide
- Bullies others
- Carries or uses weapons
- Defies authority
- Destroys property
- Deliberately annoys others
- Displays attitudes of …
  Anxiety
  Boredom
  Callousness
  Emotional emptiness
  Insolence
  Irritability
  Spite
- Engages in acts of …
  Arson
  Cruelty to people, animals
- Engages in unsafe sexual behaviors
- Fails to take responsibility
- Fidgets
- Forces sexual relations
- Forgets
- Harms others
- Harms self
- Lacks …
  Ability to focus
  Ability to keep friends
  Impulse control
  Organization habits
  Patience
- Loses …
  Temper
  Things
- Makes careless mistakes
- Manipulates others
- Performs poorly in school
- Promotes arguments and fights
- Rages
- Refuses to obey
- Resents people, events
- Resists help
- Runs away
- Self-mutilation, disfigurement
- Sinks into moods
- Skips school
- Steals
- Threatens suicide
- Throws tantrums
- Underachieves
- Unsafe sexual behavior
- Vandalizes
- Violates rules

Our goal for this workbook is NOT to diagnose a mental illness, or even for the facilitator to make that diagnosis from this book's content. Please see page ix for further explanation.

Skills that Teens Will Practice in These Modules

Module I Poor Impulse Control
Learn self-control
Identify feelings
Develop listening skills
Learn ways to focus
Build mindfulness
Identify negative thoughts
Recognize impulse triggers
Recognize impulsiveness
Identify irrational thinking
Define consequences of actions
Discover positive assertive behaviors
Manage anger

Module II Defiant Attitude
Recognize anger situations
Identify one's aggressiveness
Understand reactions to authority figures
Discover the root causes of one's defiant behavior
Learn what defiant behavior is masking
Build a conflict resolution process
Define conflicts: Where, when, why and with whom
Discover causes of conflict
Identify positive aspects of one's life
Practice positive attitude
Discover tools of joy and laughter
Define negativity and positivity

Module III Hyperactive Behavior
Overcome feelings of inadequacy
Add structure to gain control of impulses
Prioritize
Maintain attention to a single task
Channel energy in constructive ways
Understand how daydreaming interferes with focus
Learn techniques for relaxing
Define ways to limit distractions
Develop organization techniques
Reduce forgetfulness
Set and attain goals
Identify accomplishments done well

Module IV Anger and Aggression
Avoid angry and aggressive people
Affiliate with people with reasonable temperaments
Respond thoughtfully
Identify sources of stress
Understand anger triggers
Determine healthy and unhealthy outlets
Express anger in reasonable ways
Learn anti-anger tools
Deal with anger and aggression
Identify root causes of your anger
Express angry feeling
Learn about one's own aggressions
Explore your body, mind and emotions
Stop holding onto anger

Module V Erasing the Stigma of Mental Health Issues
Recognize types of mental health stigmas
Discuss disruptive behavior without judgments
Identify trusted people to talk with
Explore the effects of disruptive behavior
Understand, accept and recover
Distinguish mental illness from wellness
Explore effects of disruptive behavior on self and others
Understand a therapist can be helpful
Defy the stigma of going to a therapist
Refute stereotypes
Cope with the stigma of one's mental health issues
Improve disruptive behavior
Decrease worry about what others think
Identify personal strengths and achievements
Explore how others treat people with issues
Participate in activities
Overcome self-doubt
Identify beliefs about disruptive behavior
Illustrate how disruptive behavior looks
Refute myths about mental health issues
Overcome self-doubt
Speak out against stigmas

Specific skills for each specific activity handout are listed on the second page of each module and serve as behavioral objectives and competencies for educational and treatment plans.

Format of the *Managing Disruptive Behavior Workbook for Teens*

The *Managing Disruptive Behavior Workbook for Teens* is designed to be used either independently or as part of an established mental health program. You may administer any of the assessments and the guided self-exploration activities to an individual or a group with whom you are working over one or more days. Feel free to pick and choose those that best fit the outcomes you desire. The purpose of this workbook is to provide facilitators who work with individuals and groups with a series of reproducible activities that can be used to supplement their work with teens. Because the activity pages in this workbook are reproducible, they can be photocopied as is, or changed to suit each individual and/or group, and then photocopied.

Assessments

Assessments, with scales for each module, establish a behavioral baseline from which facilitators and teens can gauge progress toward identified goals. This workbook will supplement a facilitator's work by providing assessments designed to measure behavioral baselines for assessing client change. In order to do so, assessments with scoring directions and interpretation materials begin each module. The authors recommend that you begin presenting each topic by asking teens to complete the assessment. Facilitators can choose one or more, or all of the activities relevant to their teens' specific needs and concerns.

The awareness modules contained in this workbook will prompt insight and behavioral change and begin with a scale for the following purposes:
- Help facilitators to develop a numerical baseline of behavior, attitude, and personality characteristics before they begin their plan of treatment.
- Help facilitators gather valuable information about their teen clients/students.
- Help facilitators measure change over time.
- Help teens feel part of the treatment-planning process.
- Provide teens with a starting point to begin to learn more about themselves and their strengths and limitations.
- Facilitators may use these scales as pre-tests and post-tests to measure changes in behavior, attitude and personality.
- Facilitators identify patterns that are negatively affecting a teen.

Assessments are a great aid in developing plans for effective change and decreased disruptive behaviors. Be aware of the following when administering, scoring, and interpreting the assessments contained in this workbook:
- The purpose of these assessments is not to pigeonhole or diagnose people, but to allow them to explore various elements of themselves and their situations.
- This workbook contains *self-assessments* and not *tests*. Traditional tests measure knowledge or right or wrong responses. For the assessments provided in this workbook, remind teens that there are no right or wrong answers. These assessments ask for only opinions or attitudes.
- Assessments in this workbook have face value, but have not been formally normed for validity and reliability.
- Assessments in this workbook are based on self-reported data. In other words, the accuracy and usefulness of the information is dependent on the information that teens honestly provide about themselves. Assure them that if they don't want anyone else to know what they wrote, they do not need to share their information. They can be honest.
- Assessments are exploratory exercises and not a judgment of who the teens are as human beings.
- Assessments are not a substitute for professional assistance and/or diagnosis. If you feel any of your teens need more assistance than you can provide, refer them to an appropriate professional.

(Format continued on the next page)

Introduction

Format of the *Managing Disruptive Behavior Workbook for Teens* (Continued)

Assessment Script

When administering the assessments contained in this workbook, please remember that the assessments can be administered, scored, and interpreted by the client/student. If working in a group, facilitator can circulate among teens as they complete assessments to ensure that there are no questions. If working with an individual client/student, facilitators can use the instruction collaboratively.

Please note: It is extremely helpful for you, as the facilitator, to read and/or complete the assessment prior to distributing to the teens. As your teens begin the assessments in this workbook, the instructions below are meant to be a guide, so please do not feel you must read them word for word.

Tell your teens: *"You will be completing a quick assessment related to the topics we are discussing. Assessments are powerful tools, but only if you are honest with yourself. Take your time and be truthful in your responses so that your results are an honest reflection of you. Your level of commitment to completing the assessment truthfully will determine how much you learn about yourself. You do not need to share your assessments with anyone if you don't want to."*

Ask teens to turn to the first page of their assessment and read the instructions silently to themselves. Then tell them: *"All of the assessments have similar formats, but they have different scales, responses, scoring instructions and methods for interpretation. If you do not understand how to complete the assessment, ask me before you turn the page to begin."*

Then tell them: *"There is no time limit for completing the assessments. Take your time and work at your own pace. Do not answer the assessments as you think others would like you to answer them or how you think others see you. These assessments are for you to reflect on your life and explore some of the barriers that are keeping you from living a more satisfying life. Before completing each assessment, be sure to read the instructions."*

Ask if anyone has a question. Then tell them: *"Learning about yourself can be a positive and motivating experience. Don't stress about taking the assessments or discovering your results. Just respond honestly and learn as much about yourself as you can."*

Tell teens to turn the page and begin answering with Question 1. Allow sufficient time for all teens to complete their assessment. Answer any questions people have. It is extremely helpful for you, as the facilitator, to read and/or complete the assessment prior to distributing to the teens. As people begin to finish, read through the instructions for scoring the assessment. Have teens begin to score their assessments and transfer their scores for interpretation. Check to be sure that no one has a question about the scoring.

Review the purpose of the interpretation table included after each assessment. Tell the teens: *"Remember, this assessment was not designed to label you. Rather, it was designed to develop a baseline of your behaviors, to give you a view of where you are, at this time. Regardless of how you score on an assessment, consider it a starting point upon which you can develop healthier habits. Take your time, reflect on your results, and note how they compare to what you already know about yourself."*

After teens have completed, scored, and interpreted their assessment, facilitators can use the self-exploration activities included in each module to supplement their traditional tools and techniques to help teens learn to function more effectively.

(Continued on the next page)

Format of the *Managing Disruptive Behavior Workbook for Teens* (Continued)
Self-Exploration Activities

This workbook provides self-exploration activities after each assessment. These can be used to induce behavioral change, enhance thinking skills and decrease disruptive behavior problems. These activities are designed to prompt self-reflection and promote self-understanding. They use a variety of formats to accommodate all learning styles, foster introspection, and promote pro-social behaviors, life skills and coping skills. The activities in each module correlate to the assessments to enable you to identify and select activities quickly and easily.

Self-exploration activities assist teens in self-reflection, enhance self-knowledge, identify potential ineffective behaviors, and teach more effective ways of coping with problem behaviors. They are designed to help teens make a series of discoveries that lead to increased social and emotional competencies, as well as to serve as an energizing way to help teens grow personally and scholastically. These brief, easy-to-use self-reflection tools are designed to promote insight and self-growth.
Many different types of guided self-exploration activities are provided for you to pick and choose the activities that are most needed by your teens and the ones that will be most appealing to them. The unique features of the exploration activities make them user-friendly and appropriate for a variety of individual sessions and group sessions.

Teens will engage in the following activities:
- Explore ways they could make changes in their lives to feel better. These activities are designed to help teens reflect on their current life situations, discover new ways of living more effectively, and implement changes in their lives to accommodate these skills.
- Journal as a way of enhancing their self-awareness. Through journaling prompts, teens will be able to write about the thoughts, attitudes, feelings, and behaviors that have contributed to, or are currently contributing to, their current life situation. Through journaling, teens are able to safely address their concerns, hopes and dreams for the future.
- Explore their disruptive behavior problems by examining past behavior for negative patterns and learning new ways of dealing more effectively in the future. These activities are designed to help teens reflect on their lives in ways that will allow them to develop healthier lifestyles.

The facilitator has the choice of how to process the activities – individually, in a full group or with volunteers sharing, etc.

Introduction

IMPORTANT INFORMATION FOR FACILITATORS
When Using the *Managing Disruptive Behavior Workbook for Teens*

Our goal for this workbook is NOT to diagnose a mental illness, or even for the facilitator to make that diagnosis from this book's content. Our goal is to *touch* on some of the symptoms and possibilities, create realizations, and provide coping methods which will help people to go forward and perhaps consider the possibility of the need for consideration of medications and therapy.

Our goal is also to help teens recognize that other people have the same issues, that no shame is connected to them, and mental illness of any degree is not to be stigmatized nor should anyone need to feel like a victim of stereotyping. In this workbook, we are using the phrase *mental condition* in order to include ALL types of disruptive behavior problems, from just losing your temper some to serious mental illness.

Seek Professional Help!

Teens who experience severe bouts of disruptive behaviors may need to seek professional help from a medical/psychological professional. Some of the questions you can evaluate to determine if professional assistance is needed:

- Has the teen been experiencing these disruptive behaviors for a longer time than usual, lasting perhaps for weeks or even months?
- Are these disruptive behaviors causing bigger problems at school, on a salaried or a volunteer job, at home, or in the teen's community?
- Has the person's efforts to manage the disruptive behaviors failed?
- Does the person feel hopeless and helpless in trying to change the disruptive behavior?

Teens need to do much more than complete the assessments, activities and exercises contained in this workbook if they have serious mental issues. All disruptive behavior problems need to be thoroughly evaluated by a medical professional, and then treated with an appropriate combination of medication and group and/or individual therapy.

CONFIDENTIALITY:

Instruct teens to use NAME CODES when writing or speaking about anyone. Teens completing the activities in this workbook might be asked to respond to assessment items and journal about relationships. Before you begin using the materials in this workbook explain to teens that confidentiality is a term for any action that preserves the privacy of other people. Maintaining confidentiality is extremely important as it shows respect for others and allows – even encourages - teens to explore their feelings without hurting anyone's feelings or fearing gossip, harm or retribution.

In order to maintain this confidentiality, ask teens to assign a NAME CODE for each person they write about as they complete the various activities in the workbook. For example, a friend named **Joey** who **enjoys going to hockey games** might be titled **JLHG** (Joey Loves Hockey Games) for a particular exercise. In order to protect their friends' identities, they will not use people's actual names or initials, just NAME CODES.

Erasing the Stigma of Mental Health Issues through Awareness

The Approach

As important as it is for everyone, it is vital that facilitators keep an open mind about mental health issues and the stigma attached to the people with these issues. This series of workbooks, *Erasing the Stigma of Mental Health Issues through Awareness*, is designed to help facilitators work to diminish the stigma that affects teens experiencing disruptive behavior problems.

Stigma occurs when people are labeled which then sets the stage for discrimination, embarrassment, shame and humiliation. Facilitators are able to help erase the stigma of mental health issues through enhanced awareness of the factors that activate the issues. They can accentuate the depth of the problems, and accelerate awareness, acceptance and understanding.

To assist you, the facilitator, our fifth module in each book of this series is entitled *"Erasing the Stigma of Mental Health Issues."* It is included in this workbook to provide activities associated with difficult behavior problems.

Our thanks to these professionals who make us look good and who personify people who are dedicated to erasing the stigma of mental health issues.

Art Director – Joy Dey
Assistant Art Director – Mathew Pawlak
Editor and Lifelong Teacher – Eileen Regen
Editorial Director – Carlene Sippola
Proofreader Extraordinaire – Jay Leutenberg
Reviewer – Carol Butler, MS Ed, RN, C
Teen Reviewer – Hannah Lavoie

Introduction

Table of Contents

MODULE I – Poor Impulse Control 15
    Poor Impulse Control Scale Introduction and Directions 17
    Poor Impulse Control Scale 18
    Scoring Directions 19
    Profile Interpretation 19
    Scale Descriptions...19
    My Self-Control Log 20
    Acting on My Feelings: Ineffectively..................................21
    Acting on My Feelings: Effectively...................................22
    Listening Skills 23
    Take Your Mind Off of It!..24
    Practice Mindfulness 25
    Underlying Thoughts..26
    Impulse Triggers 27
    Impulsive Behaviors..28
    When I Act Impulsively 29
    Thinking Skills 30
    How I Felt Afterwards 31
    Assert Yourself 32
    Being Assertive 33
    Getting a Grip...34
    My Impulses 35

MODULE II – Defiant Attitude 37
    Defiant Attitude Scale Introduction and Directions 39
    Defiant Attitude Scale 40
    Scoring Directions 42
    Profile Interpretation 42
    Scale Descriptions...42
    What Happens When You Become Aggressive.............................43
    Types of Aggressiveness..45
    Unwillingness to Accept Authority 46
    Roots of Defiance 47
    Acting Out...48
    The Conflict Resolution Process......................................49
    Conflict Resolution Insight 50
    Causes of Conflict 51
    Positive Perspective 53
    Learned Positivity 54
    Removing Negativity..55
    Journaling My Thoughts...56

Managing Disruptive Behavior Workbook for Teens

Table of Contents

MODULE III – Hyperactive Behavior 57
- Hyperactive Behavior Scale Introduction and Directions 59
- Hyperactive Behavior Scale 60
- Scoring Directions 61
- Profile Interpretation 61
- Scale Descriptions 61
- Feelings of Inadequacy 62
- Gaining Control through Structure 63
- Prioritizing 64
- Maintaining Attention 65
- Channeling Energy 66
- Do You Daydream? 67
- Relaxation Techniques 68
- Distractions 69
- Organized Mess 70
- Reduce Forgetfulness 71
- Reaching Goals 72
- Overreacting 73
- Let's Get Organized 74
- Avoiding Activities 75
- Things I Do Well 76

MODULE IV – Anger & Aggression 77
- Anger & Aggression Scale Introduction and Directions 79
- Anger & Aggression Scale 80
- Scoring Directions 81
- Profile Interpretation 81
- Scale Descriptions 81
- Birds of a (Different) Feather 82
- Birds of a (Same) Feather 83
- Respond Rather than React 84
- Stressful Reactions 85
- Anger at School 86
- Anger at Home 87
- Healthy and Unhealthy Outlets 88
- Anger Expression 89
- Anti-Anger Tools 90
- More Anti-Anger Tools 91
- Acting on Anger 92
- My Anger Motives 93
- How Aggressive are You? 94
- If My Aggressive Body Could Talk 95
- Holding on to Anger 96

Introduction

Table of Contents

MODULE V – Erasing the Stigma of Mental Health Issues..........97
    Erasing the Stigma of Mental Health Introduction 101
    Two Types of Mental Health Stigma....................................102
    The Stigma of Being Known as "Disruptive" – THE PAST 103
    The Stigma of Being Known as "Disruptive" – THE FUTURE 104
    "I was a Disruptive Child" 105
    Understanding, Acceptance and Recover 106
    Illness becomes Wellness..107
    Effects of the Stigma of Disruptive Behavior..........................108
    The Stigma of Going to a Mental Health Therapist 109
    Stereotypes...110
    Coping with the Stigma of Disruptive Behavior.......................111
    Improvement 112
    My Negative Thoughts 113
    Focus on Your Strengths...114
    Ways I Am Treated..115
    Stay Active...116
    Self-Doubt...117
    A Poster about the BELIEFS Related to a Disruptive Behavior..........118
    A Poster about ACCEPTANCE of People with Disruptive Behavior.......119
    DE-STIGMA-TIZE with the Facts about Mental Health Issues............120
    Coping with the Stigma of a Mental Issue 121
    Speak Out Against Stigmas..122

MODULE I

Poor Impulse Control

He who controls others may be powerful, but he who has mastered himself is mightier still.

~ Lao Tzu

Name _____

Date _____

Managing Disruptive Behavior Workbook for Teens

Skills Emphasized in Each Activity Handout

My Self-Control Log .... page 20
Record ways one has maintained self-control for one week.

Acting on My Feelings: Ineffectively .... page 21
Identify feelings, ways one handled situations ineffectively and how one could have handled them better. Describe the connection between feelings and ineffective behaviors.

Acting on My Feelings: Effectively .... page 22
Describe feelings, situations one handled effectively, the results, and the connection between feelings and effective behaviors.

Listening Skills .... page 23
Compare in writing one's ways of listening in a specific situation to a description of listening skills.

Take Your Mind Off of It! .... page 24
Document one's impulsive actions in past situations, when and how the actions could have been interrupted.

Practice Mindfulness .... page 25
Write about a specific situation: one's thoughts, emotions, physical sensations and urges. Note what was learned through the mindfulness exercise.

Underlying Thoughts .... page 26
Identify thoughts that preceded impulsive actions. State ways one could have changed thoughts to avoid the actions.

Impulse Triggers .... page 27
Describe one's psychological and physical triggers to impulsive actions and the resultant feelings.

Impulsive Behaviors .... page 28
State situations, one's impulsive actions and consequences related to family, school, friends, relationships and other areas of life.

When I Act Impulsively .... page 29
Demonstrate insight about one's impulsive actions by completing sentence starters.

Thinking Skills .... page 30
Replace one's overly dramatic, irrational and exaggerated thoughts with more positive and rational ideas.

How I Felt Afterwards .... page 31
List times one acted impulsively, the consequences and describe related emotions.

Assert Yourself .... page 32
Depict and describe situations in which one loses control. Identify ways assertiveness would help maintain control.

Being Assertive .... page 33
Review definitions of assertive, passive, passive-aggressive and aggressive and then describe a time one acted passive and became angry. Note feelings and ways one could initially have been more assertive.

Getting a Grip .... page 34
Give examples of constructive and aggressive ways to handle anger and then identify which describes one's behavior better.

My Impulses .... page 35
Apply a quote to one's impulses by describing which impulses to obey and not to obey.

Poor Impulse Control Scale
Introduction and Directions

Impulsivity is any behavior displayed without thinking first or thinking about the consequences of a behavior. You may often find yourself behaving in an impulsive way. When this type of behavior happens occasionally, it may not be a problem. However, when you are unable to control your impulses, the behavior will begin to interfere with your effectiveness in school and in your relationships with family, friends, community contacts and employers.

You can use the following scale to explore the level of your impulsive behavior in your daily life. This assessment contains 30 statements related to your ability to control your impulses. Read each of the statements and decide how much the statement describes you.

This can help you only if you are honest in your responses to the statements in the scale.

- If the statement describes you a lot, circle the number under that column for that item.
- If the statement describes you sometimes, circle the number under that column for that item.
- If the statement describes you only a little or not at all, circle the number under that column for that item.

In the following example, the circled number under "A Lot" indicates the statement is descriptive of the person completing the inventory a lot of the time.

	A LOT	SOMETIMES	A LITTLE/NONE
I don't think before I act	(3)	2	1

This is not a test. Since there are no right or wrong answers, do not spend too much time thinking about your answers. Be sure to respond to every statement.

Turn to the next page and begin.

Poor Impulse Control Scale

	A LOT	SOMETIMES	A LITTLE/NONE
I don't think before I act	3	2	1
I blurt out words without thinking them through	3	2	1
I don't like to wait in line	3	2	1
I will take something that is not mine even though I know better	3	2	1
I will do something even if I am told not to do it	3	2	1
I often act on the spur of the moment	3	2	1
I rarely make a plan before starting anything	3	2	1
I am quick to decide on a course of action	3	2	1
I do most things recklessly	3	2	1
I get caught up in social media and post too quickly	3	2	1
I act on impulses which gets me in trouble later	3	2	1
I want to be popular and I say yes too quickly	3	2	1
I do everything in a hurry	3	2	1
I am not very cautious	3	2	1
I often say things I later regret	3	2	1
I give up when I am bored	3	2	1
I feel restless a lot of the time	3	2	1
I buy things on impulse even though I hardly need them	3	2	1
I plan very few things ahead of time	3	2	1
I do things at a moment's notice even though I know better	3	2	1
I bully others without thinking how it makes them feel	3	2	1
I make fun of others without thinking twice	3	2	1
I drive recklessly when I am in a hurry	3	2	1
I am more focused on the future than the present	3	2	1
I make up my mind too quickly	3	2	1
I am a risk taker - healthy or unhealthy risks	3	2	1
I give in to peer pressure easily	3	2	1
I don't use logic when making decisions	3	2	1
I don't wear a helmet or seat belts when I'm in a hurry	3	2	1
I drive if my friends ask me to, even if have been drinking or using drugs	3	2	1

TOTAL = _____

Poor Impulse Control

Poor Impulse Control Scale
Scoring Directions

A lack of impulse control can interfere with relationships, work, school, social activities, and participation in the community.

The *Poor Impulse Control Scale* is designed to help you explore how well you are able to control your impulses so that they do not become disruptive in your life. For the scale you just completed, add the numbers that you circled. This score will give you some sense of how well you control your impulsive behaviors. Your total will range from 30 to 90.

Then, transfer this total to the space below:

Poor Impulse Control TOTAL _____

Profile Interpretation

Individual Score	Result	Indications
30 - 49	Low	Low scores indicate a high level of impulse control. Complete the following exercises to ensure that you continue to do a good job and even improve on controlling your impulsivity.
50 - 69	Moderate	Moderate scores indicate a medium level of impulse control. Complete the following exercises to ensure that you can enhance your ability to control your impulsivity even further.
70 - 90	High	High scores indicate a very low level of impulse control. Complete the following exercises to help you learn to recognize and control your impulsivity.

The following activities are designed to help increase your level of impulse control. Regardless of how you scored on the scale, please complete all of the activities.

Scale Description

If you scored high on this assessment you tend to have a limited amount of self-control. You probably do things in a hurry and act impulsively. You don't think before you act and often say things you regret later. You do not plan ahead of time and act on the spur of the moment.

Managing Disruptive Behavior Workbook for Teens

My Self-Control Log

It is important for teens to realize how often they are able to maintain self-control rather than acting impulsively. Keep a log of when you show self-control and when you minimize negative behaviors in your mind, and when you don't act impulsively or speak negatively to others. Use NAME CODES.

Reproduce this form for multiple weeks.

Days	How I Maintained Self-Control
Monday	
Tuesday	
Wednesday	
Thursday	
Friday	
Saturday	
Sunday	

Poor Impulse Control

Acting on My Feelings: INEFFECTIVELY

In order to control impulsivity, it helps to learn more about the connection between feelings and behaviors. Experiencing a feeling and acting on the feeling are two distinct processes. *For example, feeling anger and acting on the feeling by yelling.* Think about some situations when you had strong feelings. Describe how you handled them in a way that was not effective, and how you could have handled the situation better.

The Situation	My Feelings	How I Handled the Situation Ineffectively	How I Could Have Handled It Better
Example: My girlfriend was talking to my archenemy in a very friendly way.	*I felt betrayed.*	*The minute I was alone with her I started screaming and I wouldn't listen to anything she had to say.*	*I could have walked away and calmed down and later asked her about the conversation, quietly telling her how I felt and why. I know she wouldn't have been so angry with me.*

When you are impulsive, describe the connection between your feelings and your ineffective behaviors?

_____

_____

_____

Managing Disruptive Behavior Workbook for Teens

Acting on My Feelings: EFFECTIVELY

In order to control impulsivity, teens need to learn more about the connection between feelings and behaviors. Teens must learn that experiencing a feeling and acting on the feeling are two distinct processes. *For example, feeling impatient and acting on that feeling by dealing with it in a positive way.* In this activity, think about your some of the situations in which you had strong feelings, describe how you handled them well, and the result of your behaviors.

The Situation	My Feelings	How I Handled the Situation Effectively	The Result of My Behavior
Example: I waited for half an hour to pick up a prescription at the store.	*I felt annoyed and impatient.*	*I walked up to the clerk and said I had been waiting for half an hour, my mom was waiting for me to bring it home, and I'm wondering if there is a problem.*	*The clerk said they were very busy but he'd check. He did and came back and apologized and said it would be five more minutes. It was and I thanked him.*

When you are not impulsive, describe the connection between your feelings and your effective behaviors?

_____

_____

_____

Poor Impulse Control

Listening Skills

A lack of effective listening skills may lead you to act impulsively. You may not listen to directions and act without having heard what was actually said. Following are some guidelines for listening effectively. To practice them, think about a time when you did or did not listen well to instructions.

What was the situation? _____

- **Listen to what is said and repeat it out loud before taking action.**

    Did you do this? _____ Was it effective? Explain. _____
    _____
    _____

- **Watch the person's body language for cues about important components of the message. Maintain eye contact; listen to the tone of the speaker's voice; watch posture, arm and hand movements; and notice the distance maintained by the speaker.**

    What did you notice about the person's body language? _____
    _____
    _____

- **Don't allow yourself to be distracted. Don't think about other topics, interrupt, or allow yourself to be distracted.**

    Were you distracted? _____ In what ways? _____
    _____
    _____

- **Restate key phrases to clarify their importance.**

    Did you do this, and how effective was it? _____
    _____
    _____

- **Ask the speaker to clarify anything you do not understand.**

    Were you assertive enough to ask questions? _____ If so, how did that help you?
    _____

    If not, what happened? _____
    _____
    _____

Take Your Mind Off of It!

When people act impulsively, they often act with full attention and focus. One way to derail impulsive behavior is to recognize the impulsive behavior and interrupt it. Think about some ways you could do that (writing in a journal, walking away, watching a video on the Internet, etc.). Focus on situations in which you most often acted impulsively in the past, and then think about ways you might have interrupted the behavior before it became a problem.
USE NAME CODES.

My Past Impulsive Situations	At What Point Did I Realize this isn't a Good Situation	How I Could Have Interrupted the Action
Example: I took a ride from a driver I didn't know and realized she had been drinking.	*The car was swerving and she was not looking ahead.*	*I could have said "please stop the car, I just remembered something I need to do."*

What did you discover about how you can still have control even if you begin to act impulsively?

_____

_____

Practice Mindfulness

Mindfulness is the act of bringing attention into the present moment and living in that moment without judgment. For teens, this can be very helpful in controlling impulses. For this activity, take a few seconds and simply focus your attention in the impulsive moment.

What thoughts kept going through your head?

_____

_____

_____

What feelings did you experience?

_____

_____

_____

How did your body feel?

_____

_____

_____

What urges did you experience?

_____

_____

_____

What did you learn from this experience?

_____

_____

_____

Underlying Thoughts

It is important to explore the negative thoughts that precede impulsive actions. Look at some of the times this past week when you acted impulsively and complete the table below.
USE NAME CODES.

A Time I Acted Impulsively	Thoughts that Preceeded My Actions	How I Could have Changed My Thinking to Avoid the Action
Example: I cut in front of others in the school lunch line.	I am hungry…hungrier than anyone else in this line!	The other people in line are probably just as hungry as I am.

When you are about to do something impulsively, what can you say to yourself to slow yourself down and rethink? Consider a mantra you will repeat to yourself over and over!
(For example: "slow down, you move to fast")

_____

_____

_____

Impulse Triggers

People who experience impulse control issues can learn to recognize the triggers that preceed their impulsive behavior. These impulses are usually psychological *(for example, your reaction to someone's attitude, tone of voice, or way they treat you)* **or physical** *(for example, clenched fists, sweaty palms, or clenched jaw).*

Think back and reflect on the times you have acted impulsively. In the table below discuss the psychological and physical triggers you feel before acting impulsively. USE NAME CODES.

Areas of My Life	Psychological and/or Physical Triggers	How I Felt
Example: Family	*EGR starts to yell at me.*	*I become frightened and my stomach starts to hurt. I think about running away.*
Family		
School		
Friends		
Dating		
Other		

When you feel impulse triggers, what can you say to yourself to avoid impulsive action?

_____

_____

_____

Managing Disruptive Behavior Workbook for Teens

Impulsive Behaviors

People often display impulsive behaviors at home, in school and with their friends, but they are not always aware of how often they act impulsively. It is important to explore how often you are acting impulsively.

In the table below identify how many times you acted impulsively in the past week.
USE NAME CODES.

Areas of My Life	What Happened and How I Acted Impulsively	The Consequences of my Actions
Example: Family	*MJR yelled at me and I ran away from home*	*I got in trouble with strangers I met, and then the police, went home, got grounded and suspended for a week from school. Needed to make up schoolwork.*
Family		
School		
Friends		
Dating		
Other		

What area of your life do you find yourself acting most impulsively? Why? _____

_____

_____

When I Act Impulsively ...

Think about what happens when you act impulsively. Answer the following sentence starters to learn more about yourself and your impulsive behavior. USE NAME CODES

When I act impulsively, I…

When I act impulsively, I don't have to…

When I act impulsively, people…

When I act impulsively, my friends…

When I act impulsively, I avoid…

When I act impulsively, I often…

When I act impulsively, my self-esteem…

When I act impulsively, people say I'm…

What did you learn about yourself and the outcomes of acting impulsively?

_____

_____

_____

Managing Disruptive Behavior Workbook for Teens

Thinking Skills

People often act impulsively when their thinking becomes overly dramatic, irrational, or exaggerated. By replacing negative thoughts with more positive rational ones, a person can more easily maintain control before acting impulsively.

In the spaces that follow, describe the times your thinking was overly dramatic, irrational, or exaggerated. USE NAME CODES.

My Actions	What Happened?	The End Result
Example: *Overly Dramatic*	*GRB became angry with me in school and said she'd never talk to me again. I told everyone secrets about her that were confidential.*	*I lost even more friends for being so disloyal and I ruined her reputation.*
Overly Dramatic		
Irrational		
Exaggerated		

How can you be more realistic when situations like this happen?

_____

_____

Poor Impulse Control

How I Felt Afterwards

People often can lessen their impulsive actions when they think ahead about the consequences of their actions and how they feel afterwards. List below the times you acted impulsively, the consequences of your actions, and how you felt after the action.
USE NAME CODES

Time I Acted Impulsively	Consequences of My Action	How I Felt
Example: I bullied someone who had his own problems.	He cried. He had to drop a class to avoid me. He told his parents who told my parents.	I was angry at him at first for getting me in trouble, but then I felt ashamed for affecting him so badly and adding to his problems. I felt terrible.

How can thinking about consequences affect your future actions?

_____

_____

_____

Managing Disruptive Behavior Workbook for Teens

Assert Yourself

By learning assertive behavior (not passive, not aggressive, and not passive aggressive), teens can often achieve more effective outcomes when they find themselves in situations where they lose control. For example, when encountering peer pressure to drink alcohol, a teen could assertively say that he or she doesn't need to drink alcohol to have fun.

In the spaces that follow, draw or write about four situations in which you lose control and could have been more assertive, which would to lead to positive outcomes.

SITUATION 1	SITUATION 2
SITUATION 3	SITUATION 4

How can you make a promise to yourself to do at least one of these assertive activities when you feel like you are losing control?

_____

_____

Poor Impulse Control

Being Assertive

Demonstrating assertive behavior, rather than passive, aggressive, or passive aggressive behavior can help teenagers achieve more positive outcomes without acting impulsively. By expressing themselves assertively, teens can stand up for themselves without losing control and acting impulsively.

- When you behave passively, control of your life is in the hands of other people.
- When you behave aggressively, you often feel better initially, but usually lasts only a short time and then is replaced by frustration and guilt.
- When you behave passive-aggressively, you often feel sneaky with no satisfaction.

To behave assertively, try these tips:

- Use assertive body language with direct eye contact, keep your head up and shoulders back, hands relaxed with limited hand gestures, and a calm voice.
- Take responsibility
- Use "I" statements to express your feelings
- Avoid words like "you never" or "you should have"

Now you try! In the spaces below, recall a time when you acted like a doormat (and let someone walk all over you), and then reacted with anger. USE NAME CODES.

What happened? _____

_____

What did you do? _____

_____

How did you feel? _____

_____

How did you react afterwards? _____

_____

What would have been an assertive way to act in the first place? _____

_____

Managing Disruptive Behavior Workbook for Teens

Getting a Grip

People become angry. It is a natural emotion.
The most important part about feeling angry is learning how to manage it in a constructive way (NOT aggressively).

On the lines below, list some of the constructive ways to handle anger,
and then some aggressive ways to deal with anger.

Aggressive Ways to Handle Anger

_____   _____
_____   _____
_____   _____
_____   _____
_____   _____

Constructive Ways to Handle Anger

_____   _____
_____   _____
_____   _____
_____   _____
_____   _____

Review the lists above. Which is more characteristic of you? _____

Do you have some thoughts on how you will deal with anger? _____

_____

_____

My Impulses

> *The art of living consists in knowing which impulses to obey and which must be made to obey.*
> ~ **Sydney J. Harris**

What does this quote mean to you?

_____

_____

_____

What are the impulses you should obey?

_____

_____

_____

What are the impulses you should not obey?

_____

_____

_____

How can you be sure to be able to identify the difference between these two?

_____

_____

_____

MODULE II

Defiant Attitude

You are the sum total of everything you've ever seen, heard, eaten, smelled, been told, forgot – it's all there. Everything influences each of us, and because of that I try to make sure that my experiences are positive.

~ *Maya Angelou*

Name _____

Date _____

Managing Disruptive Behavior Workbook for Teens

Skills Emphasized in Each Activity Handout

Aggression Prevention .... page 43
Describe a specific situation and the physical, mental and behavioral clues that one's anger may turn to aggression. Identify techniques to relax the body, change thoughts and adopt positive behaviors to make aggression less likely..

Types of Aggressiveness .... page 45
Describe one's aggressive behavior in four categories: verbal, emotional, physical and sexual. Identify when these types of aggression occur, why and how to stop the behaviors.

Unwillingness to Accept Authority .... page 46
State reactions to five or more types of authority figures' requests, reasons for defiant reactions, and one way to respond calmly to each request.

Roots of Defiance .... page 47
Describe experiences with nine or more possible root causes of defiance.

Acting Out .... page 48
State ways one acts out and what each behavior may be masking. Name persons who can help and why they were selected.

The Conflict Resolution Process .... page 49
Identify one's conflict situation, what both parties wanted and how they felt. Brainstorm possible compromises and solutions; then note the best resolution.

Conflict Resolution Insight .... page 50
Demonstrate insight by explaining where, when, with whom and why most of one's conflicts occur. Identify patterns that emerge and ways to stop them.

Causes of Conflict .... page 51
Rate the frequency of one's conflicts in eleven categories and explain reasons for each. Note one's most common types of conflicts and ways to avoid them.

Positive Perspective .... page 53
Depict four positive aspects of one's life; acknowledging that focus on negativity promotes defiance.

Learned Positivity .... page 54
Describe one's negative thoughts and actions in over six areas of life. Replace each with positive ways to think and act.

Removing Negativity .... page 55
Identify times of laughter and joy and how these help to remove negativity.

Journaling My Thoughts .... page 56
Journal one's personal interpretation of two quotations that promote positivity.

Defiant Attitude Scale
Introduction and Directions

Defiance is resistance to authority or open disregard for others, especially those in authority. Defiance is a common problem associated with the teen years. Therefore, it is important for you to develop awareness of the symptoms of a defiant attitude:
- Aggressive
- Rebellious
- Conflict-Prone
- Negative

This assessment contains 32 statements designed to help you explore how your defiance may be affecting the other people in your life. Read each of the statements and decide whether the statement describes you or not. If the statement does describe you, circle the number in the YES column next to that item. If the statement does not describe you, circle the number in the NO column next to that item.

In the following example, the circled 1 indicates the statement does not describe the person completing the inventory:

	YES	NO
I bully others	2	(1)

This is not a test. Since there are no right or wrong answers, do not spend too much time thinking about your answers. Be sure to respond to every statement.

Turn to the next page and begin.

Defiant Attitude Scale

	YES	NO
I bully others	2	1
I initiate fights	2	1
I lose my temper easily	2	1
I try to dominate others	2	1
I abuse others, physically, emotionally, verbally or sexually	2	1
I have violent thoughts	2	1
I have thoughts about harming animals	2	1
I threaten other people	2	1

A TOTAL = _____

I disobey adult directions	2	1
I argue with adults	2	1
I am disrespectful to teachers	2	1
I often pretend not to hear realistic rules at school	2	1
I pride myself on being rebellious	2	1
I deliberately disobey requests at home	2	1
I refuse to obey rules	2	1
I am purposely disobedient	2	1

R TOTAL = _____

(Continued on the next page)

Defiant Attitude Scale (continued)

	YES	NO
I am often in conflict situations	2	1
During conflicts, I cannot control my emotions and I cry	2	1
I don't handle conflict well, even though I may have started it	2	1
I am unable to communicate calmly in conflict situations	2	1
I am unable to minimize conflicts with others	2	1
I am unable to manage conflict situations in reasonable ways	2	1
I cannot compromise to avoid conflicts	2	1
I'm unable to control my temper in a conflict	2	1

C TOTAL = _____

I am very critical of others	2	1
Others say I have a negative attitude	2	1
I often say "It will never work"	2	1
I complain a lot	2	1
I am rarely upbeat and happy	2	1
I tend to be judgmental of others	2	1
My first thought is usually a negative one	2	1
I can't control my negative thoughts	2	1

N TOTAL = _____

Defiant Attitude Scale
Scoring Directions

The Defiant Attitude Scale you just completed is designed to measure each of the aspects that contribute to a defiant attitude. For each of the sections on the previous pages, count the scores you circled. Put that total on the line marked TOTAL at the end of each section.

Then, transfer your total to the space below:

A	=	Aggressive	TOTAL _____
R	=	Rebellious	TOTAL _____
C	=	Conflict-Prone	TOTAL _____
N	=	Negative	TOTAL _____

Add your four scores together for your Grand TOTAL _____

Profile Interpretation

Individual Score	Grand Total	Result	Indications
8 - 9	32 - 37	Low	Low scores indicate that you do not seem to have a defiant attitude. Complete the following exercises to continue your positive behaviors.
10 - 14	38 - 57	Moderate	Moderate scores indicate that you are being somewhat affected by a defiant attitude. Complete the following exercises to reduce the effects even more.
15 - 16	58 - 64	High	High scores indicate that you are being greatly affected by a defiant attitude. Complete the following exercises to reduce the effects of a defiant attitude.

Scale Description

AGGRESSIVE – People scoring high on this scale tend to be aggressive. They tend to bully and dominate others, and often lose their temper and get into fights

REBELLIOUS – People scoring high on this scale tend to be uncooperative with adults and argue with them. They are disrespectful to adults and disobey requests and rules.

CONFLICT-PRONE – People scoring high on this scale are not able to handle conflict well. They find themselves getting into conflicts with others, and are unable to control their emotions and their anger in conflict situations.

NEGATIVE – People scoring high on this scale tend to be very negative. They complain a lot, have a negative point of view, and expect the worst in most situations.

GRAND TOTAL – High scores on all four scales indicate that the person demonstrates an extremely defiant attitude. The following activities will be helpful to everyone, no matter how they scored.

Defiant Attitude

Aggression Prevention

What types of things happen when you become aggressive? Exploring the situations in which you find yourself becoming angry and the situations when that anger turns to aggressiveness can help you be aware and prepared to manage your aggression.

In the spaces that follow, describe the situations in which you find yourself becoming angry, and having that anger turn to aggression. USE NAME CODES.

With what situation or problem do you find yourself becoming angry?

What clues tells you that you are becoming angry?

My body...

My thinking ...

My behavior ...

(Continued on the next page)

Aggression Prevention *(Continued)*

How can you begin to relax your body?

How can you monitor your self-talk for negative thoughts and change them to positive thoughts?

What positive behaviors can you take on to help deal with the situation?

How can you learn from this situation and be less aggressive in the future?

Defiant Attitude

Types of Aggressiveness

Defiant teens display many different types of aggression. Aggressiveness includes negative verbal, physical, emotional and sexual behaviors. In the sections below, identify which of these four types of aggressiveness you use.

Verbal	Physical	Emotional	Sexual
☐ Threatening	☐ Punching	☐ Gossiping	☐ Unwanted touching
☐ Intimidating	☐ Hitting	☐ Excluding	☐ Ignoring "NO"
☐ Teasing	☐ Kicking	☐ Spreading rumors	☐ Stalking
☐ Mocking	☐ Slapping	☐ Rejecting	☐ Using inappropriate language
☐ Name-Calling	☐ Shoving	☐ Laughing at	☐ Posting private pictures
☐ Yelling	☐ Tripping	☐ Isolating	☐ Raping
☐ Lying	☐ Spitting	☐ Ignoring	☐ Unwanted kissing
☐ Accusing	☐ Biting	☐ Applying peer pressure	☐ Attempting rape
☐ Interrogating	☐ Scratching	☐ Humiliating	☐ Practice unsafe sex
☐ Berating	☐ Pushing	☐ Minimizing	☐ Hurling insults
☐ Withholding Info	☐ Using weapons to inflict harm	☐ Swearing	☐ Gossip about sexual encounters
☐ Raging	☐ Throwing	☐ Denying	☐ Forcing sex
☐ Bullying	☐ Pulling hair	☐ Brainwashing	☐ Betraying privacy
☐ _____	☐ _____	☐ _____	☐ _____
☐ _____	☐ _____	☐ _____	☐ _____

When do you find yourself using each or any of these types of aggression?

_____

_____

Why should you stop?

_____

_____

How can you stop?

_____

_____

Unwillingness to Accept Authority

Although teens who are defiant may not be so all the time, their defiant behavior is to be disruptive. Teens use defiant behaviors to show their unwillingness to accept authority.

In the table below, for each type of authority figures, identify what is usually asked of you. Describe how you react and why. USE NAME CODES.

Authority Figures	What They Ask of You	How you React and Why?
Example: Parents/Caregivers	*Clean my room.*	*I get angry. Scream. Refuse. I know where everything is and I like it that way. It's my room and they can close the door.*
Parents/Caregivers		
Teachers		
Legal Authority		
Siblings		
Peers		
Other		

Write something you can do differently to keep yourself calm when you react to each of the above requests:

_____
_____
_____
_____

Defiant Attitude

Roots of Defiance

The key is to provide growth is to identify some of the reasons you may be acting defiantly. It is often difficult to discover the exact causes, but it is important to explore some of the root causes that may be triggering your defiant attitudes and behaviors. People who show a defiant attitude may have a variety of reasons. For each of the items below, describe your experience. If any of these do not apply to you, just skip them. USE NAME CODES

Rejection by my peers

Learning issues

Sibling issues

Past or present abuse

Home issues

Physical issues

Emotional issues

Mental health issues

Thinking defiance is a cool attitude

Other

Acting Out

Many defiant teens act out to mask other problems, such as family abuse, trouble in school, social life, etc. Think about what your defiant behavior might be masking. Complete the table that follows. USE NAME CODES

How I Act Out	What I Am Masking	Who is a Trusted Person I Can Talk to So I Can Make My Situation Better. Why This Person?
Example: I am the 'class clown,' always smiling, making jokes, even when the teacher is talking.	I am so very, very sad. My family is breaking up.	I can talk to MPC. He will listen and not judge my family and me.

If you do not have someone to talk with that you feel you can trust, consider speaking with a favorite teacher, school counselor or clergy person.

Defiant Attitude

The Conflict Resolution Process

Coping with conflict is a process that anyone can learn. By learning this process, people can ensure positive outcomes with their conflict situations. Think about a conflict you had recently. Work through the process below to see if you could have achieved a different outcome.

Conflict Situation _____

What did you want from this situation?
_____
_____
_____

What did the other person want from this situation?
_____
_____
_____

How did you feel about the situation?
_____
_____
_____

How did the other person feel?
_____
_____
_____

Using this information, now brainstorm several possible solutions to the conflict in which both of you would compromise so that you both would benefit.
_____
_____
_____
_____
_____
_____

Best Solution: _____

Conflict Resolution Insight

Insight is important in every part of your life, and certainly important in your management of your conflicts. Think about the times that you find yourself in conflict with other people, and complete the following sentences. USE NAME CODES

WHERE do your conflicts occur? My conflicts occur …	**WHEN do your conflicts occur?** My conflicts occur …
WITH WHOM do your conflicts occur? My conflicts occur with …	**WHY do most of your conflicts occur?** My conflicts occur because …

What patterns do you see emerging? How can you put an end to them?

_____

_____

_____

Defiant Attitude

Causes of Conflict

Following are some of the more common causes of teen conflicts. For each cause place an X on the line to show the frequency of conflicts in this category. Next, write a short statement below the line to explain or describe why and/or how these conflicts occur.

1) **Desire to develop your own identity**

          Not Many Conflicts   **Many Conflicts**

          0--------------------------------5--------------------------------10

2) **Need for independence**

          Not Many Conflicts   **Many Conflicts**

          0--------------------------------5--------------------------------10

3) **Authority**

          Not Many Conflicts   **Many Conflicts**

          0--------------------------------5--------------------------------10

4) **Bullying**

          Not Many Conflicts   **Many Conflicts**

          0--------------------------------5--------------------------------10

5) **Parents/Caregivers rules**

          Not Many Conflicts   **Many Conflicts**

          0--------------------------------5--------------------------------10

6) **Sibling Rivalry**

          Not Many Conflicts   **Many Conflicts**

          0--------------------------------5--------------------------------10

(Continued on the next page)

Causes of Conflict (continued)

7) Not doing home/schoolwork

        Not Many Conflicts   **Many Conflicts**

        0-------------------------------5-------------------------------10

8) Being unreliable

        Not Many Conflicts   **Many Conflicts**

        0-------------------------------5-------------------------------10

9) Engaging in dangerous/illegal activities

        Not Many Conflicts   **Many Conflicts**

        0-------------------------------5-------------------------------10

10) Discipline/Rules

        Not Many Conflicts   **Many Conflicts**

        0-------------------------------5-------------------------------10

11) Lack of understanding/Poor communication

        Not Many Conflicts   **Many Conflicts**

        0-------------------------------5-------------------------------10

What did you notice about the types of conflicts you get into the most?

_____

_____

_____

How can you avoid getting into so many conflicts?

_____

_____

_____

Defiant Attitude

Positive Perspective

Some people tend to live their lives from a negative perspective. This can contribute to a defiant attitude. Rather than fixating on the negative, try to look at the positive, bright side of life. In the spaces that follow, draw the most positive aspects of your life. This could include accomplishments, personality traits, relationships, etc.

Learned Positivity

Believe it or not, you can learn to be more positive in your life. Think about ways that you can begin to see various aspects of your life in more positive ways.

In the table below, identify your negative ways of thinking and acting, and then describe ways you can be more positive. USE NAME CODES

Aspects of My Life	My Negative Thinking and Acting	More Positive Ways of Thinking and Acting
Example: Home	*They won't give me the car whenever I want it. I act furious because I am furious. They don't trust me/ They think I'm not old enough to drive.*	*I do know that they need the car too. I can negotiate for times when they're not using it. I know they do trust me. It's just inconvenient.*
Parents / Caregivers		
School		
Work / Volunteer		
Peers		
Dates		
Commuity		
Other		

Defiant Attitude

Removing Negativity

The best way of removing negativity is to laugh and be joyous.
~ **David Icke**

What does this quote mean to you? _____
_____
_____
_____

How did you feel when reading this quote? _____
_____
_____
_____

When do you laugh? _____
_____
_____
_____

Give an example and the results. _____
_____
_____
_____

When are you joyous? _____
_____
_____
_____

Give an example and the results. _____
_____
_____
_____

If you are willing share examples with others in the room.

Journaling My Thoughts

You can learn a lot about your own negativity from journaling about famous quotes.
What do the following quotes mean to you?

*We can complain because rose bushes have thorns,
or rejoice because thorn bushes have roses.*

~ Abraham Lincoln

_____
_____
_____
_____
_____
_____
_____
_____
_____

No matter what you're going through, there's a light at the end of the tunnel and it may seem hard to get to it but you can do it and just keep working towards it and you'll find the positive side of things.

~ Demi Lovato

_____
_____
_____
_____
_____
_____
_____
_____
_____

MODULE III

Hyperactive Behavior

*I'm sorry … I wasn't
paying attention
to what I was thinking.*

~ Shelley Curtiss

Name _____

Date _____

Managing Disruptive Behavior Workbook for Teens

Skills Emphasized in Each Activity Handout

Feelings of Inadequacy .... page 62
Identify ways one feels inadequate and the reasons. Provide proof that the inadequacies are inaccurate and state what was learned.

Gaining Control through Structure .... page 63
Demonstrate ways to gain control through structure by drawing or doodling four or more techniques that apply to oneself from a list of ten suggestions.

Prioritizing .... page 64
Practice prioritizing by listing one's tasks, selecting the most important task, breaking it into four manageable steps, specifying a schedule and noting ways to avoid becoming distracted.

Maintaining Attention .... page 65
Describe three ways one becomes distracted and the effects. Identify solutions for each using a list of eight suggestions and adding one's own ideas.

Channeling Energy .... page 66
Identify twelve or more ways one's high energy can be productive. State how one felt before and after each activity.

Do You Daydream? .... page 67
State where, when and with whom one daydreams. Describe insights about what is happening within oneself, daydreaming purposes and its effects.

Relaxation Techniques .... page 68
Review three techniques, practice deep breathing and meditation and describe their benefits. Assess the types of exercise and time spent each week.

Distractions .... page 69
Illustrate insight about internal and external distractions by depicting what one is doing when distracted, where and with whom, and the nature of the distractions.

Organized Mess .... page 70
Describe a potential mess in one's life, its level of organization or disorganization, and what to do if it is causing a problem.

Reduce Forgetfulness .... page 71
Name four or more places where one is forgetful and describe when, what is most forgotten, why, and the effects of forgetfulness.

Reaching Goals .... page 72
State one's goals in three or more areas, define obstacles and ways to achieve goals. Identify which goal to meet next, the target date, and ways to continue the goal-oriented behavior.

Overreacting .... page 73
Demonstrate calm reactions by describing disappointments, how one may have over-reacted loudly or violently, and how one could have reacted in calmer ways.

Let's Get Organized .... page 74
Plan organized task completion by defining the task, describing its implementation plan, breaking it into four steps and evaluating the process.

Avoiding Activities .... page 75
State four activities one avoids, why, and the results. Select one and describe a plan to devote time and attention to the activity.

Things I Do Well .... page 76
Identify what one does well in five or more aspects of life, ways to expand the activities and which are most enjoyable.

Hyperactive Behavior Scale Introduction and Directions

While all people have a hard time focusing and being attentive, some teens experience these difficulties in disruptive ways at home, in school, and with their peers. These teens often have difficulty maintaining their attention, organization plan and impulses. Many teens are unable to stop moving around and have trouble staying seated and keeping quiet. The purpose of this assessment is to determine the extent to which your hyperactive behavior is being disruptive to yourself and others around you.

Read each statement carefully and decide if the statement is related to your hyperactive behavior or not.

- If the statement describes you **a lot**, circle the number 3 next to the statement in that column.
- If it describes you **somewhat**, circle the number 2 next to the statement in that column.
- If it describes you a **little or not at all**, circle the number 1 next to the statement in that column.

Complete all of the items before going back to score the assessment.

In the following example, the circled 2 indicates that the statement has some effect on the person completing the scale.

	A LOT	SOMEWHAT	A LITTLE/NONE
I get distracted	3	(2)	1

This is not a test and there are no right or wrong answers. Do not spend too much time thinking about your answers. Your initial response will be the most true for you. Be sure to respond to every statement.

Turn to the next page and begin.

Hyperactive Behavior Scale

	A LOT	SOMEWHAT	A LITTLE/NONE
I get distracted	3	2	1
I become bored before I finish most things	3	2	1
I fail to finish tasks before moving on to something else	3	2	1
I am distracted by new things	3	2	1
My attention is easily diverted	3	2	1
I am easily sidetracked	3	2	1
My mind is often elsewhere	3	2	1

I – TOTAL = _____

	A LOT	SOMEWHAT	A LITTLE/NONE
I am disorganized	3	2	1
I am forgetful	3	2	1
I make careless mistakes	3	2	1
I appear not to listen when spoken to	3	2	1
I frequently lose things	3	2	1
I daydream a lot	3	2	1
I have trouble paying attention to tasks	3	2	1

II – TOTAL = _____

	A LOT	SOMEWHAT	A LITTLE/NONE
I don't pay attention to details	3	2	1
I have trouble following directions	3	2	1
I cannot remember things	3	2	1
I cannot follow through on tasks	3	2	1
I cannot organize tasks or activities	3	2	1
I forget daily chores	3	2	1
I have trouble processing information	3	2	1

III – TOTAL = _____

	A LOT	SOMEWHAT	A LITTLE/NONE
I speak out before others can respond	3	2	1
I have trouble sitting still	3	2	1
I am unable to wait my turn	3	2	1
I constantly fidget and squirm	3	2	1
I talk excessively	3	2	1
I have difficulty being quiet	3	2	1
I am always on the go	3	2	1

GO TO THE SCORING DIRECTIONS		IV – TOTAL = _____

Hyperactive Behavior Scale
Scoring Directions

Add the numbers you circled on the scales and write those scores on the lines marked TOTAL. Then, transfer those totals to the spaces below and add them together for your scale score:

I	=	Distraction	TOTAL _____
II	=	Focus	TOTAL _____
III	=	Details	TOTAL _____
IV	=	Motive	TOTAL _____
			Total Scale SCORE _____

Profile Interpretation

Individual Score	Grand Total	Result	Indications
7 - 11	28 - 46	Low	Low scores indicate that you do not experience much hyperactivity in your life.
12 - 16	47 - 65	Moderate	Moderate scores indicate that you experience some hyperactivity in your life.
17 - 21	66 - 84	High	High scores indicate that you experience a great deal of hyperactivity in your life.

Total scales score indicate the level of hyperactivity.

No matter how you scored, low, moderate or high, you will benefit from these exercises.
By going to the next section and completing the activities that follow, you will define ways to control your hyperactive behavior.

Scale Descriptions

DISTRACTION People scoring high on this scale are easily distracted by external sights, activities and sounds.

FOCUS People scoring high on this scale have difficulty sustaining attention to tasks and projects.

DETAILS People scoring high on this scale fail to give close attention to details and they make careless mistakes in school, work, and other activities.

MOTIVE People scoring high on this scale often fidget with their hands or squirm in their seat. They have difficulty being quiet and may talk excessively. They are restless and need to be constantly moving around.

Feelings of Inadequacy

Teens who are always in motion and have a difficult time focusing often feel inadequate about themselves. In the spaces that follow identify those ways in which you feel inadequate and then list reasons to prove that each item is not accurate.

Ways I Feel Inadequate	Why I Feel This Way	Proof to the Contrary
Example: *I'm not good in school*	*I have a hard time concentrating*	*I earned an A in Math*

What have you learned about yourself and your "adequacies"?

_____

_____

_____

Hyperactive Behavior

Gaining Control through Structure

A sense of structure is critical in the success of anyone who wants to be less hyperactive and have fewer disruptive behavior problems. Many teens struggle with low frustration tolerance, following rules, and impulsiveness. By adding structure, you will feel less overwhelmed in your physical environment.

- Break tasks down into smaller steps
- Don't procrastinate and put things off until later
- Give yourself more time than you think you will need
- Keep up with a calendar and planner
- Maintain as much organization in your life as possible
- Make lists and notes to keep track of important details and projects
- Practice time-management skills
- Prioritize
- Reward yourself for each accomplishment
- Study in an area with no distractions

How can you add more structure to your life?
In the spaces that follow, draw or doodle ways you will add structure.

Stick with the systems you set up!

Managing Disruptive Behavior Workbook for Teens

Prioritizing

Many teens who struggle with impulse control, tend to jump from task to task and project to project, never finishing any of them. Learning to prioritize tasks can help you to complete one task or project before moving on to the next one. Here is a system for prioritizing your tasks and projects. Think about all of the tasks and projects you need to complete next week and list them:

_____

_____

_____

_____

Step 1: Decide what to do first – What is the most important task or project to complete first?

_____

Why did you prioritize this one first?_____

Step 2: Break things down – In this step, you will break down the larger task or project above into smaller, more manageable steps. Now you try:

Begin: _____

_____

Next: _____

_____

Next: _____

_____

Next: _____

_____

Step 3: Stay Focused – In this step, you will need to find ways to stay on track and not get sidetracked. Set a specific schedule and state ways to avoid being distracted:

Date_____   Begin _____

Date_____   Next _____

Date_____   Next _____

Date_____   Next _____

Now, get started!

Hyperactive Behavior

Maintaining Attention

Teens often have a hard time focusing and maintaining their attention on a single subject or task, especially if it is one that is not of interest to them. Several tips that you can use to maintain your attention:
USE NAME CODES

- Find a place to work where you can concentrate with no distractions.
- Jot ideas on a piece of paper to be looked at later.
- Find something about each task or subject that interests you so that you can maintain your focus longer.
- Ask for written instructions you can view at a later time.
- Write down instructions and directions.
- Repeat verbal directions aloud so that you are sure to get them correct.
- Take breaks at appropriate times.
- Maintain regular routines for doing chores, completing homework, etc.

Ways I Get Distracted	How It Affects Me	My Solution
Example: When I do homework at the kitchen table.	Everyone walks in and talks. I don't get my work done, and then I get in trouble.	Find a place in the house where I know I won't be disturbed.

How will these solutions help you maintain your attention?

_____

_____

Managing Disruptive Behavior Workbook for Teens

Channeling Energy

Hyperactive teens are easily distracted because they have way too much energy. Their high energy, if properly channeled in constructive ways, can be very productive. However, they must determine how to effectively channel all of their energy.

In the spaces that follow, identify types of activities in which you have already tried to channel your energy. State how you felt before engaging in them and how you felt afterwards.

Ways I Channeled Energy	How I Felt Before	How I Felt Afterwards
Walk or jog		
Write, Draw, Paint, Craft, etc.		
Ride a bicycle		
Dance		
Skateboard		
Swim		
Hike		
Ski, Toboggan, Skate, etc.		
Play Sports		
Do Chores around the House		
Work out, Aerobics, Exercise		
Join Clubs in School		
Other		
Other		

List three from the list above that you haven't done before, or haven't done for a long time, and that you will try.

1) _____

2) _____

3) _____

Do You Daydream?

When you daydream, your attention wanders to other events or people while you are trying to focus. You stop listening and drift away into your own thoughts or fantasies.
USE NAME CODES

In what situations do you usually find yourself daydreaming?

_____
_____
_____

When you find yourself daydreaming what are you trying to escape or avoid?

_____
_____
_____

When you find yourself daydreaming, are you alone or with anyone in particular? Whom?

_____
_____
_____

What conclusions can you come to about when, where, and with whom you are, when you begin daydreaming?

_____
_____
_____

What are the effects of your daydreaming?

_____
_____

Managing Disruptive Behavior Workbook for Teens

Relaxation Techniques

Relaxation can be of great benefit to anyone who displays hyperactive behavior. Consider a variety of techniques that may help you relax. You can find many relaxation techniques on reliable Internet sources.

Deep Breathing – Deep breathing involves inhaling slowly through your nose (you should notice your abdomen going out and in) and exhaling through your mouth. Repeat this process by continuing to take long, slow deep breaths that raise and lower your abdomen. Continue this process for at least five to ten minutes or until your mood has lightened. Now you try it. Then describe below how you felt during and after the deep breathing exercise.

_____

_____

_____

Exercise – Exercise can help you to release excessive energy, stay calm, and fight the symptoms of hyperactivity. List the types of exercise you get each week and how much time you put into these exercises.

_____

_____

_____

How can you add variety and/or devote more time to exercise each week?

_____

_____

Meditation – Meditation can help you to focus your attention on one thing at a time and keep outside interferences away. For example, you could take a few minutes and gaze at an object of your choice (a candle, cup, flower, etc.) at your eye level. Gaze at the object for a few minutes. Note its size, shape and color. If you become distracted, simply return your gaze to the object. You could also count your breaths by counting one for each time you inhale and two when you exhale. Continue counting your breaths until you reach ten, and then begin again with one.

Try it and state in which situations you could use meditation.

_____

_____

_____

Distractions

Distraction occurs when your attention is set on something internal to you (headaches, worry, hunger) or external to you (traffic, whispering, others talking).

Doodle about those times when you find yourself distracted:
What are you doing? Where are you? Who is with you? What distracts you?

Organized Mess

> *My room may be a mess
> but it's an organized mess.
> I know right where
> everything is.*
> ~ **Brandon Curtiss**

What else in your life is a mess, other than your room?

_____
_____
_____
_____
_____

Is your mess an organized mess or do you know *right where everything is*? Explain.

_____
_____
_____
_____
_____

Is it causing you a problem? _____ If so, what can you do about it?

_____
_____
_____
_____

Hyperactive Behavior

Reduce Forgetfulness

All people forget things. Forgetting once in a while is typical of ordinary behavior. However, when you begin forgetting important things on a more consistent basis, it is important to explore when and where you are forgetful and how forgetfulness affects you.

In the spaces below, write about what you forget and the effect forgetfulness has on you.
USE NAME CODES

Where I am Forgetful	When I am Forgetful	What I Forget Most	How This Affects Me
School	*History class*	*Class assignments*	*I don't do what I am supposed to do and then I get in trouble at school and at home*
School			
Home			
On a Job			
With My Friends			
Other			

In each category, think about why you believe you are forgetful in that particular situation.

School _____

Home _____

On a Job _____

With My Friends _____

Other _____

Managing Disruptive Behavior Workbook for Teens

Reaching Goals

Some teens have a difficult time setting attainable goals and working toward them. Goal setting requires teens to be patient, think about the big picture, and gauge their success over time. In the spaces that follow, list your goals and the steps you will take to achieve these goals. Goals might include "I'm going to earn a B in English this term" or "I'm going to complete all my chores at home next week."

Areas of My Life	Goals	Obstacles	Steps I Will Take
Home	*Set the table for dinner*	*I get home late sometimes*	*Either be home one-half hour early to set the table or set the table after breakfast.*
Home			
School			
Job			
Other			

What goal do you want to reach next? _____

_____

What day or date will you do it? _____

_____

How will you remember to keep it up? _____

_____

Hyperactive Behavior

Overreacting

Sometimes teens get frustrated when they are disappointed or life does not go the way they expect. They overreact loudly or violently.

Think about some of the situations that trigger violent reactions to disappointments.
In the space that follows, list the disappointments you experienced this week and how you reacted.
How could you have reacted more calmly? USE NAME CODES

Disappointments	How I Reacted	How I Could Have Reacted in a Calmer Way
Example: *I didn't make the soccer team.*	*I punched a hole through the wall*	*I could have talked with the coach and asked what I need to work on to make the team next year.*

In what situations do you find yourself overreacting?

_____

_____

Managing Disruptive Behavior Workbook for Teens

Let's Get Organized

Teens often have difficulty organizing tasks, developing an implementation plan, and carrying out multiple steps.

Identify a large task you must complete, describe how you will develop a plan for completing the tasks, and identify steps for carrying out your plan. USE NAME CODES

Task to be organized: _____

_____

_____

Plan for completing the task: _____

_____

_____

_____

_____

Steps to take to complete the task:

Step #1 _____

_____

Step #2 _____

_____

Step #3 _____

_____

Step #4 _____

_____

Evaluation of your success: _____

_____

_____

Hyperactive Behavior

Avoiding Activities

Teens often avoid certain activities that require continual concentration and attention.

What activities do you avoid because they will require more attention and focus than you can give, or because you simply have very little interest in them? USE NAME CODES

Activities I Avoid	Why I Avoid this Activity	The Results of Avoiding this Activity
Example: *Visiting MGM*	*I have so little extra time and she wants to tell me so many stories about her life.*	*I barely see her and she gets hurt feelings and thinks I don't love her.*

Choose one of the activities that you avoid from your above list. Make a plan to define how you will complete the activity in a way that you can give it your full attention. (Example: Tell MGM you will see her once a month, every Sunday at 2 p.m., for a whole hour.)

_____

_____

_____

Managing Disruptive Behavior Workbook for Teens

Things I Do Well

Teens who are unable to control their attention and disruptive behaviors often feel as if they are not good at doing anything at all. In the spaces that follow, list those things you do well in different aspects of your life.

Aspect of My Life	What I Do Well	How I Can do More of This
Example: Arts, Crafts, Write, Dance, etc.	*I play the guitar very well and even write some of my own music.*	*I can offer to play at parties and maybe I can find a band to play with.*
Home		
School		
Work / Volunteer		
Sports / Exercise		
Arts, Crafts, Write, Dance, etc.		
Other		

What activities do you enjoy AND do well?

_____

_____

MODULE IV

Anger & Aggression

Speak when you are angry and you will make the best speech you will ever regret.

~ Ambrose Bierce

Name _____

Date _____

Managing Disruptive Behavior Workbook for Teens

Skills Emphasized in Each Activity Handout

Birds of a (Different) Feather .... page 82
Identify people in one's life who are angry and aggressive. Describe the aggressive behavior. Note what one has done to protect oneself. State ways to distance oneself from each aggressive person.

Birds of a (Same) Feather .... page 83
Surround oneself with people who deal with stress in a reasonable way by naming those who do not resort to anger and aggression. Describe the positive ways these people deal with stress. State ways to spend more time with these positive role models.

Respond and React with Care .... page 84
Plan ways to respond thoughtfully, rather than react in anger, by sharing past situations and how one reacted. State what one could have done to reduce anger and aggression and how this can help in the future.

Stressful Reactions .... page 85
Identify sources of stress in five or more areas of one's life. Explain why each leads to anger. State positive ways to deal with the stress and anger.

Anger at School .... page 86
Demonstrate anger awareness and ability to express one's feelings verbally by completing eleven sentence starters about school-related stressors.

Anger at Home .... page 87
Identify independence-related conflicts and other issues at home that lead to anger. State how one typically reacts.

Healthy and Unhealthy Outlets .... page 88
Differentiate between healthy and unhealthy outlets for anger and aggression by comparing one's healthy and unhealthy outlets at home, school, with friends and in the community. Identify ways to actively participate in beneficial hobbies, physical and recreational activities.

Anger Expression .... page 89
Journal about situations, thoughts and feelings that result in angry and aggressive reactions. Use these insights to identify ways to better manage anger.

Anti-Anger Tools .... page 90
Review instructions then practice using two anti-anger tools. Describe one' additional techniques.

More Anti-Anger Tools .... page 91
Select tools one has used from a list of more than twelve possibilities. Describe how these tools have worked. Identify which new tools one will try within the next month.

Acting on Anger .... page 92
Identify four possible root causes of anger by journaling responses to prompts about threats and frustrations one may be experiencing.

My Anger Motives .... page 93
Express feelings about a recent angry episode by explaining the desired outcome, the actual outcome and how one could have better handled the situation.

How Aggressive are You? .... page 94
Define one's types of aggression and pinpoint the settings in which they occur using a comprehensive selection of possibilities. State the situations and settings in which one is most aggressive.

If My Aggressive Body Could Talk .... page 95
Quote what one's body, heart and brain would say when angry.

Holding on to Anger .... page 96
Describe how one holds onto anger and how this hurts. Identify ways to express anger more constructively. State ways to let go of resentment.

Anger & Aggression Scale
Introduction and Directions

Anger is a universal emotion experienced by everyone, regardless of culture or age. For teens, anger and aggression are often part of their everyday lives. It is revealing for teens to explore the intensity and the amount of angry and aggressive outbursts.

The *Anger & Aggression Scale* can help you explore the amount of angry and aggressive flare-ups you experience and gauge the intensity of those flare-ups.

This scale contains 25 statements. Read each of the statements and decide how descriptive the statement is of you. In each of the choices listed, circle the number of your response to the right of each statement.

In the following example, the circled 1 indicates that the statement is not at all descriptive of the person completing the inventory:

	A LOT OF THE TIME	SOME OF THE TIME	RARELY	NEVER
I throw temper tantrums	4	3	2	(1)

This is not a test and there are no right or wrong answers. Do not spend too much time thinking about your answers. Your initial response will be the most true for you. Be sure to respond to every statement.

Turn to the next page and begin.

Anger & Aggression Scale

	A LOT OF THE TIME	SOME OF THE TIME	RARELY	NEVER
I throw temper tantrums	4	3	2	1
I get frustrated easily	4	3	2	1
I get angry about the least little thing	4	3	2	1
I argue with adults	4	3	2	1
I am vindictive toward others	4	3	2	1
I am sad and irritable	4	3	2	1
My anger affects my work in school	4	3	2	1
I can be hostile toward others	4	3	2	1
I feel like a victim	4	3	2	1
I hold a grudge against people I get angry with	4	3	2	1
I don't tolerate frustration well	4	3	2	1
I get into trouble with my teachers or other adults	4	3	2	1
I vandalize property	4	3	2	1
I get into fights	4	3	2	1
I bully others	4	3	2	1
I am cruel to other people or animals when I am angry	4	3	2	1
I argue with authority figures	4	3	2	1
I disrespect others	4	3	2	1
I am considered aggressive	4	3	2	1
I deliberately annoy others	4	3	2	1
When I am angry I take unsafe risks	4	3	2	1
I am violent when I am angry	4	3	2	1
I do not communicate calmly when I am angry	4	3	2	1
I throw, kick, and/or punch anything when I'm angry	4	3	2	1
When I am angry I want to harm myself	4	3	2	1

TOTAL = _____

Anger & Aggression Scale
Scoring Directions

Measure the level of your anger and aggression and define ways to manage them.

Count the scores you circled and place that number on the line marked TOTAL at the end of the assessment. Then, transfer your total to the space below:

Anger & Aggression TOTAL _____

Profile Interpretation

Individual Score	Result	Indications
25 - 50	Low	Low scores indicate that you exhibit no or low bouts of anger and aggression.
51 - 75	Moderate	Moderate scores indicate that you exhibit some bouts of anger and aggression.
75 - 100	High	High scores indicate that you exhibit intense bouts of anger and aggression.

Regardless of how you scored on the assessment, you will benefit from the anger management activities that follow.

Scale Description

If you have high scores you typically have trouble managing your anger and aggression. You probably get into verbal arguments, physical fights and are hostile towards others. You may bully others, respond cruelly, and try to physically hurt people or animals.

Birds of a (Different) Feather

One way to begin overcoming your anger and aggression is to stop surrounding yourself with others who are angry, and begin hanging around others with more reasonable temperaments. Who are the people in your life who are angry and/or aggressive?   USE NAME CODES

Friend or Acquaintance	How is This Person Angry and/or Aggressive?	What have You Done about This Behavior?	How I Can Distance Myself
Example: GWB	She kicks cats when she sees them on the streets	I told her if she continued to do it I wouldn't go anywhere with her. She laughed.	I won't go anywhere with her.

If it will be difficult distancing yourself from these people, talk to a trusted adult, counselor or teacher for advice. Who might that be? USE NAME CODES

_____

_____

_____

Anger & Aggression

Birds of a (Same) Feather

To overcome your anger and aggression, it might be helpful to be friends with people who can help you develop more positive ways of dealing with the stress in your life. Who are the people in your life who are good role models and who deal with stress in ways that do not spark anger and aggression? USE NAME CODES

Friend or Acquaintance	How This Person Deals with Stress
Example: SLM	If he gets upset with someone he calmly tells the person how he feels.

How can you go about spending more time with these people?

_____

_____

_____

Managing Disruptive Behavior Workbook for Teens

Respond and React with Care

When someone responds and reacts angrily, it may appear to be defensive, and arguments and/or fights can happen. When someone responds and reacts with careful thoughts, it will be accepted more easily. To be effective in life, you need to learn how to respond and react carefully when you begin to feel angry. The choice of how to react to the emotion of anger is totally up to you. In the spaces that follow, think back to recent times when you reacted in anger. Describe those times, and then describe how you could return to a less angry state. USE NAME CODES

Angry Situation	How I Reacted	What I Could Have Done
Example: I got mad when my friend could not go to the movies.	I told her that she and I were no longer friends.	I could have asked why she was unable to go to the movies. She may have had a great reason.

What did you learn that can help you in future anger situations?

_____

_____

Stressful Reactions

Often times when people get angry, they are merely reacting poorly to stress. Therefore, it is important to identify your sources of stress.

In the table below, identify your sources of stress and how you can reduce your stressful situations.
USE NAME CODES

Areas of your Life	Why This Makes Me Angry	What I Can Do About it
Example: Home – My parents are pressuring me to go to college.	*It's my life … I'm not sure I want to go to college.*	*Sit down and talk to them about my future dreams.*
Home		
School		
Friends		
Community		
Work		
Other		
Other		

Anger & Aggression

Managing Disruptive Behavior Workbook for Teens

Anger at School

Your school setting is a place where you spend a lot of your time. It is also a place where you will feel a lot of stress, and where you may become angry and aggressive. Awareness of your feelings is an important life skill to learn. Teens often keep their feelings inside rather than learning to express them. In order to be aware of anger and express it effectively, you need to understand why you become angry.

Complete these sentence starters about things that anger you. If the sentence starter doesn't apply to you, just skip it. USE NAME CODES

I become angry when my teacher _____

When I'm upset with a school rule _____

I become angry when other students _____

I have a problem when sports teachers or coaches _____

The rules for _____ *are* _____

The security at school _____

When _____
I _____

The school hours _____

Bullies _____

Other students _____

On the bus _____

Other _____

You do not need to share this page with anyone.

Anger & Aggression

Anger at Home

Many teens become angry at home. Because they are trying to promote their own independence, they may get into arguments and fights with others at home.

When completing the sentence starters below, think about the situations at home that trigger your anger and aggression. USE NAME CODES

I become angry when my parents/caregivers _____

_____

When family members _____

_____

When I'm given rules like _____

I _____

When I'm asked to _____

I _____

When I'm expected to _____

_____

When I'm not allowed to _____

I _____

When I am grounded, I _____

_____

When unreasonable orders are given to me, I _____

_____

When _____

_____

I _____

_____

I hate when _____

_____

I mind when _____

_____

You do not need to share this page with anyone.

Managing Disruptive Behavior Workbook for Teens

Healthy and Unhealthy Outlets

It is often a challenge to find healthy outlets for your anger and aggression, but it's worth the search.

In the table below, explore healthy ways to channel your anger into hobbies, physical and recreational activities, and social activities. USE NAME CODES

Areas of your Life	Why This Makes Me Angry
In School I …	In School I …
At home I …	At home I …
With my friends I …	With my friends I …
In my community I …	In my community I …

What can you do to actively participate in more healthy outlets?

School _____

Home _____

With my friends _____

In my community _____

Anger & Aggression

Anger Expression

Learning to express your anger in reasonable ways is a sign of maturity. One way to do so is expressing your emotions through a journal. Journal about anger using the following sentence starters. USE NAME CODES

I get so angry at _____ because _____

_____

_____

_____

I hate it when_____

_____

When this happens I feel_____

I think about _____

_____

_____

I get aggressive when _____

_____

_____

_____

_____

When _____ happens, I got extremely angry because _____

_____

_____

_____

_____

Now that you realize when this happens, how can you manage that anger in a better way?

_____

_____

_____

Managing Disruptive Behavior Workbook for Teens

Anti-Anger Tools

The way you react is probably a habit formed over time. When you are beginning to feel angry or aggressive, you need to have a variety of tools in your toolbox to immediately reduce your feelings before you act on them. Try both of these tools by yourself or with a friend.

Use Empathy

Chances are that you are angry at a person or people who make rules you dislike or whose beliefs and values differ from yours.

Place a check mark in front of the statements you can apply to someone with whom you are often angry:

- ☐ They're doing the best they can do at this moment.
- ☐ Even if I believe they are wrong, my response and reactions can be calm and assertive.
- ☐ They may have emotional, physical, family or other problems right now.
- ☐ I can see them as someone in need and not make life worse for them.

Power of Positive Self-Talk

When you begin to feel yourself getting angry or aggressive, you can use the power of positive self-talk to reduce your feeling significantly.

Statements such as the following can help you to reduce the intensity of your feelings:

- *"Easy does it….you don't need to be so upset!"*
- *"I am in control."*
- *"I do not need to be so aggressive."*
- *"It's not worth it – calm down!"*

Now you try!

What other Anti-Anger Tools do you have in your toolbox?

_____

_____

_____

_____

_____

Anger & Aggression

More Anti-Anger Tools

Even though it is very complex, anger can be managed effectively. Therefore, it is important to learn a variety of tools that you can rely on when you feel angry. Here are some tools. Place a check mark in front of those you have already tried. Use the space under the tool to describe how it worked for you. USE NAME CODES

- ☐ Next time you begin to feel angry, just say to yourself that this is just a minor annoyance.

- ☐ Find a place to sit quietly by yourself for a few minutes.

- ☐ Talk with a trusted adult or counselor about your anger issues.

- ☐ Try to determine what sets your anger off and avoid those situations if possible.

- ☐ Eliminate caffeine, tobacco, illegal substances and alcohol.

- ☐ Before judging people, try giving them the benefit of the doubt.

- ☐ Find ways to express your angry feelings in positive terms.

- ☐ Find healthy ways to let off steam. (Exercise, walk, etc.)

- ☐ Avoid other people who have angry emotions and aggressive behavior.

- ☐ Communicate with others in an assertive way.

- ☐ Never be spiteful or seek vengeance for something someone does to you.

- ☐ Focus your anger on the situation or the problem, but not on other people.

- ☐ If you ever want to hurt yourself, or another person, find a trusted adult to talk with, seek counseling immediately, or call 911.

Place a star in front of the tools you will try within the next month.

Acting on Anger

Anger is often the result of threats to you, and frustrations you may be experiencing. Explore why and how you experience anger.

This activity will help you to identify the root causes of your anger. In the spaces that follow, journal your thoughts. USE NAME CODES

I am angry when things are not the way I think they should be.
In your picture of the world, what is not the way it should be?

_____

_____

_____

I am angry when I am forced to do things I don't want to do.
What types of things are you forced to do that you don't want to do?

_____

_____

_____

I am angry when I feel abandoned.
In what situations have you felt, or do you feel, abandoned?

_____

_____

_____

I am angry when I feel controlled by others, and not personally in control.
In what situations does this apply to you?

_____

_____

_____

Anger & Aggression

My Anger Motives

Being more aware of your feelings is a valuable life skill to learn. Teens often keep their feelings inside rather than learning to express their feelings. In order to be aware of anger and express it effectively, you need to understand what makes you angry. USE NAME CODES

Think about a recent situation when you became angry. What was it? _____
_____
_____

What did I want? _____
_____
_____

What was the opposition to my goal? _____
_____
_____

What was my desired outcome? _____
_____
_____

What actually happened? _____
_____
_____

What would have satisfied me? _____
_____
_____

How could I have handled it better? _____
_____
_____
_____

Managing Disruptive Behavior Workbook for Teens

How Aggressive are You?

Aggression is difficult to define, but most people think that it is inflicting physical damage people or property. Aggression can actually be distressing or harmful emotionally, physically, verbally or sexually to the recipient. Types of behaviors that may be considered aggressive are below. Circle those that describe you and list the setting (home, school, community, work/volunteering, dating, friends, other).

Abusive phone calls, letters, online messages _____

Bullying_____

Damage against property _____

Emotional, physical, verbal and/or sexual abuse _____

Harassment _____

Harming others _____

Harming self _____

Hurting animals_____

Insensitive comments _____

Intimidating others _____

Personal insults and name calling_____

Posturing and threatening gestures _____

Sarcasm_____

Setting fires _____

Shouting _____

Stealing _____

Swearing _____

Verbal threats _____

Violent acts against people _____

In what settings and situations are you most aggressive?

_____

_____

_____

_____

Anger & Aggression

If My Aggressive Body Could Talk

**Think about how your body feels when you are aggressive.
If your body could talk, what would it say?**

For each of the statements below, write about what you think your body might say.

If my body could talk, it would say …

_____
_____
_____
_____
_____
_____
_____
_____

If my heart could talk, it would say …

_____
_____
_____
_____
_____
_____
_____
_____

If my brain could talk, it would say …

_____
_____
_____
_____
_____
_____
_____
_____

Managing Disruptive Behavior Workbook for Teens

Holding on to Anger

> *Holding on to anger is like grasping a hot coal with the intent of throwing it at someone else; you are the one who gets burned.*
> ~ **Buddha**

How do you hold on to your anger? _____
_____
_____
_____
_____

How has this hurt you? _____
_____
_____
_____
_____

How can you begin to express your anger more constructively? _____
_____
_____
_____
_____

How can you begin to let go of the resentment? _____
_____
_____
_____
_____

MODULE V

Erasing the Stigma of Mental Health Issues

Stigma's power lies in silence. The silence that persists when discussion and action should be taking place. The silence one imposes on another for speaking up on a taboo subject, branding them with a label until they are rendered mute or preferably unheard.

~ M. B. Dallocchio

Name _____

Date _____

Managing Disruptive Behavior Workbook for Teens

Skills Emphasized in Each Activity Handout

Erasing the Stigma of Mental Health Issues Introduction ....page 101
Acquire information about erasing stigmas by reading and discussing: definitions, examples, effects, and ways to combat stereotypes and stigmas associated with disruptive behavior.

Two Types of Mental Health Stigma...page 102
Name incidents in which one felt stigmatized; Identify each occurrence as social and/or perceived stigma using the definitions provided.

The Stigma of Being Known as "Disruptive" – THE PAST ....page 103
Identify people in each of five or more categories with whom one has discussed disruptive behavior. Quote what was said, the persons' reactions and one's feelings. Identify possible reasons for any negative reactions.

The Stigma of Being Known as "Disruptive" – THE PRESENT ....page 104
Name trusted people in five or more categories with whom to discuss disruptive behavior Quote what one would say and the expected reactions. Identify potential gains and/or losses. Brainstorm about when in a serious relationship to discuss disruptive behavior.

"I Was a Disruptive Child" ....page 105
Use a famous athlete's revelation that helps erase the stigma. State self-assessments re: whether one is disruptive, examples, feelings and what would help decrease disruptive behaviors. Identify a person, who will listen and help, with whom to share these insights.

Understanding, Acceptance and Recovery ....page 106
Demonstrate one's understanding, acceptance and recovery from disruptive behavior by writing responses to prompts about a popular author's quotation.

Illness becomes Wellness..page 107
Explain one's concepts of mental illness and wellness. Describe someone who personifies wellness. State what it takes to personally personify wellness.

Effects of the Stigma of Disruptive Behavior...page 108
Elaborate on ways one has been affected by the stigma of disruptive behavior from a list of eight situations. Identify a person in each situation who will be supportive and give reasons for the choices.

The Stigma of Going to a Mental Health Therapist ....page 109
Identify one's pre-conceived ideas about therapy. Designate facts one was unaware of from a list of sixteen truths. Identify one's worries about talking to a therapist. Sign a written commitment to see a counselor or therapist.

Stereotypes ....page 110
Describe ways one defies each of four or more stereotypes about disruptive behavior. Compose a statement to enlighten people who label oneself with these and other stereotypes.

Coping with the Stigma of Disruptive Behavior..page 111
Describe ways to handle people who treat one differently. Name people with whom one is comfortable and uncomfortable providing self-disclosure and education. Share insights about managing one's own behavior. Celebrate other aspects of one's identity by writing about special qualities and the gifts one can offer the world.

Improvement...page 112
Personalize the concept that improvement starts with oneself by specifying ways to improve one's own behavior. Identify ways to personally spread the word to erase the stigma. Brainstorm additional ways the group can erase the stigma of people who have disruptive behavior problems.

(Continued on the next page)

Erasing the Stigma of Mental Health Issues

Skills Emphasized in Each Activity Handout *(continued)*

My Negative Thoughts ....page 113
> Identify one's negative assumptions about what others think about one's behavior. Use a physical act and visualization to avoid worries about what others think.

Focus on Your Strengths..page 114
> Demonstrate awareness of one's strengths in five aspects of life. State ways to share one's strengths and exemplify a capable and talented human being.

Ways I Am Treated ....page 115
> Describe how others treat one unfairly in six specified situations. Explain ways one treats oneself unfairly and fairly.

Stay Active ....page 116
> Identify the importance of participating in enjoyable activities by stating activities one stopped, the reasons, the effects, and ways to resume involvement.

Self-Doubt ....page 117
> Review information about stigma, self-doubt, lack of understanding and resultant feelings. Specify five aspects of one's self-doubt, its effects and actions to improve self-concept. Describe ways to overcome one's biggest self-doubt.

A Poster about the BELIEFS Related to a Disruptive Behavior ....page 118
> Creatively, depict and describe personal beliefs about how one with disruptive behavior looks when being stigmatized.

A Poster about ACCEPTANCE of People with Disruptive Behavior ....page 119
> Creatively, depict and describe how one with disruptive behavior looks when accepted by others.

DE-STIGMA-TIZE with the Facts about Mental Issues ....page 120
> Educate oneself by reading and discussing eight myths about mental illness and their corresponding facts, with emphasis on the importance of medical help for people who seem to have symptoms.

Coping with the Stigma of a Mental Health Issue ....page 121
> Personalize six coping skill suggestions by describing how one can implement each of them.

Speak Out Against Stigmas..page 122
> Identify ways one can speak out against stigmas at events, through newspaper articles, Internet blogs and other methods. List the ideas one would promote. Identify ways others and oneself will benefit from these messages.

Erasing the Stigma of Mental Health Issues
Introduction

A stigma is extreme social disapproval of some type of personal characteristic or a belief that is not considered socially "acceptable." People who have a particular attribute considered unwanted by society are rejected or stigmatized as a result of the attribute. People who are angry, defiant and impulsive are often judged unfairly to be violent, unpredictable, explosive and unstable. These judgments, or social stigmas, can cause people who display these behaviors to feel devalued as human beings. They are often ostracized from activities, rejected in social situations, stereotyped, minimized in school, home, workplace, and shunned by others. People experiencing the stigma of disruptive behavior problems often feel extreme physical and psychological distress.

People who stigmatize and/or stereotype others bring about unfair treatment rather than help. This unfair treatment can be very obvious. For example, people make negative comments or laugh. On the other hand, this unfair treatment can be very subtle. For example, people assume that a person with disruptive behavior problems is dangerous or violent, and they avoid or shun that person.

Stigmas affect a large percentage of people throughout the world. Some of the more common stigmas are associated with physical disabilities, mental health issues, age, body type, gender, sexual orientation, nationality, religion, family, ethnicity, race, religion, financial status, social sub-cultures and conduct. Stigmas set people apart from society and produce feelings in them of shame and isolation. People who are stigmatized are often considered socially unacceptable and they suffer prejudice, rejection, avoidance and discrimination.

WHAT CAN BE DONE?
Fear of judgment and ridicule about disruptive behavior often compels individuals and their families to hide from society rather than face criticism, shunning, labeling and stereotyping. Instead of seeking treatment, they struggle in silence. Let's discuss some ways you can combat the stereotypes and stigmas associated with disruptive behaviors.

- You and your loved ones have choices. You can decide who is to know more about the behavior and exactly what to tell them. You need not feel ashamed or embarrassed.
- You are not alone. Remember that many other people are coping with a similar situation.
- Seek help and remember that the activities in this workbook and treatment from medical professionals can help you to have a productive education and career and live a satisfying life.
- Be proactive and surround yourself with supportive people – people you can trust. Social isolation is a negative side effect of the stigma linked to disruptive behavior. Isolating yourself and discontinuing enjoyable activities will not help. Perhaps you and others can start a support group to share with each of your issues and solutions.

HOW CAN THIS SECTION HELP ME?
Managing Disruptive Behavior Workbook for Teens is designed to help you deal more effectively with your disruptive behaviors, and this section, Erasing the Stigma of Mental Health Issues is specifically designed to help you overcome the stigma attached to disruptive behavior problems. Complete the activities that follow to feel better about yourself, feel content, and become more resilient in the face of stress in your life.

Managing Disruptive Behavior Workbook for Teens

Two Types of Mental Health Stigma

Mental health stigma can be divided into two types:

1. **Social stigma** is characterized by prejudicial attitudes and discriminating behavior directed towards individuals with mental health issues.
2. **Perceived stigma** is the internalizing of prejudicial attitudes by the people with mental health issues, and of their understanding of discrimination.

Name some incidents when you felt people were judging you, talking about you or discriminating against you because of your behavior. Next to your description of the incident, mark a number 1 or number 2, to indicate whether it was a social stigma or a perceived stigma. If you're not sure which, mark it with a question mark.

USE NAME CODES

_____
_____
_____
_____
_____
_____
_____
_____
_____
_____
_____
_____
_____
_____
_____
_____
_____
_____
_____
_____

Often one perceives others' stigmatizing behaviors, or exaggerates others' or their own reactions.

Erasing the Stigma of Mental Health Issues

The Stigma of Being Known as "Disruptive" – THE PAST

Many different types of behaviors are disruptive! Teens tend to go through a stage of life in which they are experiencing biological, as well as psychological, changes, and disruptive behaviors emerge.

Often the stigma attached to a behavior issue stops one from moving forward, because the person feels unable to talk about it, for fear of being judged or labeled. We can erase the stigma of any mental health issues by starting to discuss them with one person at a time, and taking the time to explain thoughts and feelings.

Let's start with people with whom you have already shared. USE NAME CODES

With whom have you discussed your disruptive behaviors?	What did you say?	What was this person's reaction? What did the person say?	How did you feel?
Family			
Friends			
Acquaintances			
Teachers, Coaches and/or Other School Administrators			
School Counselor and/or Mental Health Professional			
Other			

If any one of the above reacted in a negative way, to what do you attribute that reaction?

_____

_____

_____

The Stigma of Being Known as "Disruptive" – THE PRESENT

People have perceptions about people who are disruptive. One of the ways to erase these stigmas is to talk about disruptive issues and let others know that people who tend to be disruptive are just like anyone else who have some type of an issue.

Perhaps it is time to talk with other people you trust and/or with whom you feel safe. USE NAME CODES

Person with whom you might discuss your disruptive behaviors?	What would you say to this person?	What do you think this person's reaction might be?	What could you gain and/or lose by discussing it with this person?
Family			
Friends			
Acquaintances			
Teachers, Coaches and/or Other School Administrators			
School Counselor and/or Mental Health Professional			
Other			

Brainstorm with the group:
At what point in a serious relationship is it time to discuss your disruptive behaviors?

"I Was a Disruptive Child"

> *I was a disruptive child.* ~ **Allyson Felix**
>
> Allyson Felix is an American track and field sprint athlete
> who competes internationally for the USA.

Are you disruptive? How? _____
_____
_____
_____

How does your behavior make you feel? _____
_____
_____
_____

How do others feel about your behavior? _____
_____
_____
_____

What would help you to be less disruptive? _____
_____
_____
_____

Who can you tell that to? Who is someone who will listen and help you? _____
_____
_____
_____

Understanding, Acceptance and Recovery

Journal your thoughts about the following quotation and how you can do your part to erase the stigma of disruptive behavior:

Understanding is the first step to acceptance and only with acceptance can there be recovery.
~ **J.K. Rowling**

How does this quotation pertain to your behavior? _____
_____
_____
_____

What do you need to understand? _____
_____
_____
_____

What do others in your life need to understand? _____
_____
_____
_____

What do you need to accept? _____
_____
_____
_____

What do you need others in your life to accept? _____
_____
_____
_____

What recovery do you see in your future? _____
_____
_____
_____

Erasing the Stigma of Mental Health Issues

Illness becomes Wellness

Journal your thoughts about the following quotation and how you can do your part to erase the stigma of disruptive behavior:

Never give up on someone with a mental illness. ~ **Shannon L. Alder**

What is your concept of a mental illness? _____
_____
_____
_____

What is your concept of a mental illness _____
_____ _____
_____
_____

What is your concept of wellness? _____
_____
_____
_____

Do you know someone who personifies wellness? USE NAME CODE
_____

What is it about this person that encourages you feel this way? _____
_____
_____
_____

What would it take for you to personify wellness?_____
_____
_____
_____
_____

Managing Disruptive Behavior Workbook for Teens

Effects of the Stigma of Disruptive Behavior

Check out these harmful effects of the stigma of being a person with disruptive behavior problems and write on the lines next to each item how it has affected you.
USE NAME CODES

1. Getting into fights _____

2. Lack of friends _____

3. Lack of understanding by teachers, coaches and/or other school administrators
   _____

4. People at home are often angry with me _____

5. Inability to join clubs or organizations _____

6. Bullying; physical, emotional, verbal or sexual abuse or harassment _____
   _____

7. Peer pressure from friends _____

8. The belief that you will never be able to succeed or that you can't improve your situation.
   _____

On the line of the corresponding number, write the name of a person you can speak to, a person who might help to support you about each of the situations you noted above. Add a reason you've chosen that person.

1. _____
2. _____
3. _____
4. _____
5. _____
6. _____
7. _____
8. _____

Erasing the Stigma of Mental Health Issues

The Stigma of Going to a Mental Health Therapist

Many people have pre-conceived ideas about anyone seeking therapy.
Do you know of anyone who has gone to a mental health therapist? USE NAME CODES and write what you know about the experience. _____

_____

_____

Here are some facts about mental health and mental health therapy.
- ☐ Mental health includes how you act, feel and think in different situations.
- ☐ Mental health problems can be caused by many different things including medical health issues, abuse (emotional, physical, verbal, sexual), stress, worry, loss of a relationship, food issues, self-injuries, ADHD, STD's, family changes, addictions, a traumatic event, problems, wanting to build up self-confidence, etc.
- ☐ If someone goes to a mental health therapist, this does NOT mean the person is crazy. Twenty percent of teens have mental health issues. Doctors and mental health therapists treat people the same as any other doctor treats problems (broken leg, diabetes, cancer, etc.).
- ☐ There needs to be a good connection between you and the therapist. Your therapist should be someone you feel you can trust.
- ☐ This might take a few meetings and/or a few therapists, to find the right one for you.
- ☐ Non-judgmental people who truly care about you will not judge you in a negative way. They will be proud of you for seeking help.
- ☐ The therapist does not assume that you have a mental illness. The therapist assumes something is troubling you, knows that no one leads a perfect life, and admires you for trying to make changes in your life.
- ☐ The therapist's job is to help you understand what's going on.
- ☐ The therapist will not tell you how to live your life, or how to think, act or believe.
- ☐ The therapist is not an advice-giver, but will help you think about how to increase your quality of life.
- ☐ The therapist may have some thoughts, and with you, will help you make changes.
- ☐ The therapist can help you to increase your life management skills.
- ☐ The therapist will help you recognize and express your feelings in a healthy way.
- ☐ The only person who can "fix" your problems is you, but a therapist will help you with an action plan.
- ☐ The mental health therapist may suggest that you see a medical doctor for medication.
- ☐ Therapy can be a slow or long process. Being open and honest, and wanting to feel better, will make the difference.

Place an X by the facts that you were not aware of.

What worries you about talking with a mental health therapist? _____

_____

_____

After learning about these facts, can you make a commitment to speak with a counselor or therapist?

Signature _____ Date _____

Managing Disruptive Behavior Workbook for Teens

Stereotypes

Social stigmas about disruptive behavior often translate to the following inaccurate stereotypes:

In the table below, write about how you are unlike the stereotype provided.

Stereotype	How I Defy that Stereotype
Example: People who are disruptive should be kicked out of school.	*I am still in my same school and have excellent teachers and counselors who help me a lot with their patience and direction.*
People who are disruptive should be kicked out of school	
People who are disruptive can never complete anything	
People who are disruptive are a danger to society	
People who are disruptive are bullies	
Other stereotypes of disruptive people	

What would you like to say to other people who label you with these or other stereotypes?

_____

_____

_____

_____

_____

Erasing the Stigma of Mental Health Issues

Coping with the Stigma of Disruptive Behavior

The stigma of having a disruptive behavior is often more damaging than the behavior itself. Although we have progressed quite a bit, the acceptance of mental health issues is still a long way off.

Learning to cope with your disruptive behaviors and the stigma that surrounds them will be helpful. USE NAME CODES

People treat you a bit differently. They might think of you as fragile. They do not know what will happen when someone, who has a disruptive behavior will act out, and they might avoid you altogether. What can you do about that?

_____

_____

If you would consider educating them about your behavior, what could you say?

_____

_____

Use your own discretion. It is important for you and your well-being to be educated about your behavior issues and to decide whether, and with whom, to share and/or educate. Trust your instinct. Educate and share with others with whom you feel most comfortable and can trust.

_____

_____

With whom are you comfortable talking about your behavior issues and why? _____

_____

_____

With whom are you not comfortable talking about your behavior issues and why?

_____

_____

Own your behavior. Learn how to educate yourself about your behaviors, manage them and cope with them. What do you already know about your behavior? _____

_____

_____

Accept that you are special, worthwhile and have much to offer the world. Despite your disruptive behavior, what is special about you and what do you have to offer to the world?

_____

_____

_____

Improvement

Journal your thoughts about the following quotation and how you can do your part to erase the stigma of disruptive behavior:

Improvement begins with 'I'.
~ **Arnold H. Glasgow**

How can you improve your behavior?

_____
_____
_____
_____
_____
_____
_____

How can you get the word out to erase the stigma about a disruptive behavior problem?

_____
_____
_____
_____
_____
_____
_____

Brainstorm with a few other people about how your group can get the word out to erase the stigma.

_____
_____
_____
_____
_____
_____
_____

Erasing the Stigma of Mental Health Issues

My Negative Thoughts

You can begin to overcome the stigma of being disruptive by working on your behavior and not worrying about what others will think. When you are worried about what others say about you, or might say about you, you will have constant thoughts that stop you from doing something to help yourself, even though you know you need to take action.

What are the negative thoughts that go through your head about others and what they think of you?

Others think I am …

Others don't think I can …

Others probably find me …

I think others might be afraid or wary of me because …

Others label me as …

This makes me feel …

Now that you have written these thoughts, take a big heavy black marker and put a big **X** through all of the thoughts above. When these negative thoughts come into your head, picture that big X, reminding you not to worry about what others think.

Focus on Your Strengths

You can do many things to help fight the stigma associated with disruptive behavior problems. You can focus on your strengths rather than your limitations. Demonstrate to others and yourself that you have a great deal to offer.

In the spaces that follow, identify some of your strengths. You have much to share, so take a few minutes to think about and write about some of your greatest strengths.
USE NAME CODES

My strengths related to school:

_____

_____

My strengths related to relationships with others:

_____

_____

My strengths related to my work or volunteer job:

_____

_____

My strengths related to creativity:

_____

_____

My strengths related to special skills I possess:

_____

_____

How can you share these strengths to show others that even though you may have disruptive moments, you are a capable, talented human being?

_____

_____

Erasing the Stigma of Mental Health Issues

Ways I Am Treated

Think about some of the ways that people treat you because of your disruptive behavior. In the spaces below, explore the various ways people treat you. Write about those who you feel treat you unfairly and why. USE NAME CODES.

I am rejected by family … *(example: MSE calls me names.)*

I am rejected by my friends …

I encounter problems at school …

I encounter problems at home …

I am subjected to physical violence or harassment …

I am laughed at …

I treat myself unfairly by …

I treat myself fairly by …

Stay Active

Hiding away from other people because of your disruptive behavior does not help, nor will it show other people that people who have disruptive behavior problems need support and understanding. It is important to remain active and continue participating in enjoyable activities.

In the table below, identify some of the activities you enjoy, but have stopped engaging in and why.
USE NAME CODES

Activity	Why I Stopped Doing It	How This Affected Me	How This Affected Me
Example: I joined the choir	*I became angry and yelled at the director when I wasn't chosen for a solo.*	*The director told me if I couldn't calm down, I needed to leave. I left.*	*Work on my behavior issues. Apologize to the director and ask about rejoining.*

Erasing the Stigma of Mental Health Issues

Self-Doubt

Don't let stigma create self-doubt and shame. One of the most important ways to minimize the stigma of disruptive behavior is to explore how one doubts oneself. Self-doubt almost always stems from a lack of understanding rather than from information based on the facts. Feeling ashamed, embarrassed or humiliated because of a disruptive behavior issue can be very destructive.

How does your disruptive behavior cause you to doubt yourself and how can you control your self-doubt in positive and strong ways? USE NAME CODES

Ways I Doubt Myself	How This Negatively Affects Me	What I Can Do About it
Example: How can I possibly ever go to college?	*I don't plan on taking college courses or even care about high school graduation.*	*Talk to my school counselor and get the name of a therapist help me to work on my behavior issues. College is my goal.*

What is your biggest self-doubt and how can you overcome it?

_____

_____

_____

Managing Disruptive Behavior Workbook for Teens

A Poster about the BELIEFS Related to a Disruptive Behavior

Below, draw a collage of pictures, symbols and/or words, of your beliefs of how you and your disruptive behavior look when you are being stigmatized by others.

Erasing the Stigma of Mental Health Issues

A Poster about ACCEPTANCE of People with Disruptive Behavior

In the space that follows, draw a collage of pictures, symbols and/or words, of how you and your disruptive behavior look when you are accepted by others.

DE-STIGMA-TIZE with the Facts about Mental Health Issues

Myth: Mental health issues are rare.

Fact: Mental health issues are not rare and affect nearly everyone either directly or indirectly.

Myth: People with mental health issues are unable to lead successful, productive lives.

Fact: Most people with a mental health issue respond to treatment, learn to cope with and manage their problems, and go on to lead productive and fulfilling lives.

Myth: People who have mental health issues will not get better.

Fact: Once diagnosed, mental health issues are treatable. While they are not always cured, they can be managed effectively. Most people with mental health issues live productive and positive lives while receiving treatments for their mental health issues. As is the case with any mental health issues, individuals with severe or persistent mental health issues who respond poorly to available treatments may require more support and may not function as highly as others.

Myth: People with mental health issues are violent and unpredictable.

Fact: While some people who suffer from mental health issues do commit antisocial acts, it does not equal criminality or violence - despite the media's tendency to emphasize a suspected link. People with mental health issues are no more likely to commit violence than anyone in the general public, but they are more likely to be victimized and are more likely to inflict violent behaviors on themselves.

Myth: Mental health issues happen because of bad parenting or personal weakness.

Fact: The main risk factors for mental health issues are not bad parenting or personal weakness but rather genetics, severe and prolonged stress (such as physical or sexual abuse), or other environmental influences (such as birth trauma or head injury).

Myth: Treatment for mental health issues is not usually effective.

Fact: The effectiveness of any treatment depends on a number of factors including the type of mental health issue and the particular needs of the individual. A combination of psychiatric medication and psychotherapy, or social interventions are the most effective way to treat mental health issues.

Myth: Mental health issues are caused by everyday stressors.

Fact: It may seem that stress is responsible for mental health issues; however, there is no one clear cause of these issues. Rather, it is a result of complex interactions between psychological, biological, genetic and social factors. Stress, stigma, and lack of support can make it worse on the individual.

Myth: Mental health issues are always hereditary.

Fact: Some mental health issues include a genetic component, which results in a predisposition or vulnerability toward the illness among children and siblings, but environment also plays a key role in the development of certain mental health issues. If someone in a person's family has a mental health issue, that person will be at higher risk.

If you start to experience the symptoms of a mental health issue, it is important for you to see a medical professional to determine if you have a problem that will require treatment. If you know of anyone who seems to have symptoms of a mental health issue, urge that person to do the same.

Erasing the Stigma of Mental Health Issues

Coping with the Stigma of a Mental Health Issue

Get treatment. Don't let the fear of being labeled with a mental health issue prevent you from seeking help. Treatment can provide relief by identifying and reducing symptoms that interfere with your work and personal life. How can you get treatment?

_____
_____
_____

Don't let stigma create self-doubt and shame. If you are buying into the stigma, you will have the mistaken belief that your condition is a sign of personal weakness, or that you should be able to control it better. How can you have less self-doubt?

_____
_____
_____

How can you have less shame?

_____
_____
_____

Don't isolate yourself. Have the courage to confide in your family members, friends, dating partner, clergy, school counselor or other members of your groups and/or community. Who can you reach out to and who can you trust for the compassion, support and understanding you need?

_____
_____
_____

Remember that you are not your issue. So instead of saying "I am a disruptive person," say "I am a person who is experiencing a disruptive behavior problem." In what ways do you equate yourself with your issue?

_____
_____
_____

Get help at school. If you are having disruptive behavior problems that affect your learning, find out what plans and programs might help. Who could you talk to about getting help at your school?

_____
_____
_____
_____
_____

If you and others are willing share responses.

Speak Out Against Stigmas

Speaking out about stigmas can help instill courage in others who are facing disruptive behaviors, and it will help to educate the public about the effects that impulsivity, anger, and aggression have on you personally. Speaking out for and about yourself advocates for others who might have disruptive behavior problems, and it can be beneficial to you at the same time. Think about some of the ways that you might let your voice be heard to educate others about stigmas and their damaging effects on people. For each of the items, list the ways that you could speak out against stigmas.

Express your opinions at events. What events are planned at your school where you might speak out against stigmas?

_____

_____

At what events in your community might you volunteer to speak out against stigmas?

_____

_____

You could write an informative feature article or letter to the editor of a local newspaper or your school newspaper. What would you say?

_____

_____

You could blog about stigmas on the Internet. How can you do this? _____

_____

_____

What are some other ways to speak out against stigmas? _____

_____

_____

How do you think this will benefit others? _____

_____

_____

How will it benefit you? _____

_____

_____

Whole Person Associates is the leading publisher of training resources for professionals who empower people to create and maintain healthy lifestyles. Our creative resources will help you work effectively with your clients in the areas of stress management, wellness promotion, mental health and life skills.

Please visit us at our web site: **www.wholeperson.com**. You can check out our entire line of products, place an order, request our print catalog, and sign up for our monthly special notifications.

Whole Person Associates
800-247-6789